what
HAPPENS
next?

what HAPPENS *next?*

ANSWERS ABOUT

THE AFTERLIFE

JADE-SKY

ROCKPOOL

NOTE: Names of people in this book have
been changed to protect their privacy.

A Rockpool book
PO Box 252
Summer Hill
NSW 2130
Australia

rockpoolpublishing.com

Follow us! f ⓘ rockpoolpublishing
Tag your images with #rockpoolpublishing

First published in 2010 by Rockpool Publishing
under ISBN: 9781921295324

This edition published in 2024 by Rockpool Publishing
ISBN: 9781922785466

Design and typesetting by Sara Lindberg, Rockpool Publishing

 A catalogue record for this
book is available from the
National Library of Australia

Printed and bound in China
10 9 8 7 6 5 4 3 2 1

Contents

How to use
this book

The questions that I have answered in this book are those I'm asked time and time again. They are drawn not only from clients I have read for, but also from friends, audience members at public appearances and even people I've encountered casually. To illustrate the questions and answers, I have also included true stories both from my personal experiences and from helping others connect with the spirit world.

Everyone is affected by the death of a loved one at some stage in their life, whether it's the loss of a family member, a close friend or a beloved pet. My book is designed as a simple guide to help you find the information and reassurance you seek. Turn to the topics you are interested in and I'm sure you will be comforted by the answers you find.

Introduction: my journey

How did it all start, this extraordinary yet ordinary life I lead? My earliest memories are of being in my cot in the old house that I lived in with my parents and my two older brothers. I must have been around two years old.

I remember seeing light shows above me each night: bright flashes of coloured light that were my own beautiful night-time ritual. The colours ranged from light pinks to light blues and they all melded into one. I still vividly recall those nights and the unique happiness I felt as I lay there. Looking back, this is my earliest memory of having spirits around me.

I remember, too, that the walls made a lot of noise – scratching and murmuring. When I was four or five, I would often cry out to my parents that the room was far too noisy and I couldn't sleep. The noises would go on all night long and, much to my parents' frustration, I would often end up in their bed. They said that it must be mice in the walls of the old house, but if that was the case, there must have been mice in every house I've ever lived in, because to this day this is what I hear if I don't protect myself or close myself off psychically before I sleep. I know now that the noise is spirit people talking around me during the night. They can be very noisy when they want to be.

The spirits in our home were very strong. I often had three spirits around, but my favourite spirit was also my best friend, Carly. She was the same age as me and we did everything together. When my brothers were off playing their games in the backyard or in their bedroom, I wasn't lonely because I would play tea sets or games with Carly. She looked very like me: small for her age with mousy brown hair that curled at the back.

My family was used to Carly: my mother would give her a tea cup and set a place at the dinner table for her, and all hell would break loose if one of my brothers accidentally sat on Carly at the table or on a lounge chair. To my parents, Carly was the kind of imaginary friend that many little children have, and if it kept me happy and quiet there was no harm in it. (I'm sure my 'imaginary friend' often frustrated my brothers, but I guess that's what little sisters are for.) To me, however, Carly was a living, breathing little girl who understood everything about me and my family. She would tell me funny stories and understand when I was cranky at my brothers for not including me in their games.

When I was seven or eight, we moved to a newer, brick house just up the road from our old home. I felt safe in this new house and for the first time I began to sleep quite well without the fear of hearing the 'mice' all night long. I think, too, that this is when I started to learn how to close myself off from Spirit, as I was now attending the local Catholic convent primary school. It was my life – I loved having friends and learning new things. Slowly Carly began to disappear until I could barely remember her, as my waking moments were now full of experiences with my living friends at school.

For the next few years, life was as it should be for any young girl – happy and fairly uneventful. Few memories to do with Spirit stand out from this

time, although I recall that my senses were highly attuned to the energy of those around me and I sometimes sensed something about the energy of a person that made me want to avoid them.

One such person was a family acquaintance. When I was five or six, this man came to watch me in a ballet recital. Afterwards, my mother told me to go and sit on his lap and give him a cuddle, but my legs felt as heavy as lead. I didn't want to go near him. I was very scared by his energy and didn't trust him.

Of course my parents were upset – they didn't want me to be rude – but I just could not move towards him. I was terrified and crying. It was not the first time I had come across that energy, but it was the first time I can remember being old enough to express what I did and didn't want to do.

A few years later I came into contact with this particular man again, an experience that justified my distrust of him.

When I was about twelve, I went with my family to a function at the man's home. After we'd been at the function for a while, he suggested taking me and about four other, much younger, children out in his boat.

As soon as I heard this suggestion, my whole body became rigid and I went on high alert. A voice inside my head told me not to go. I tried to tell my parents that I didn't want to go on the boat, but they said it would be fun. I could help with the younger children and watch that they didn't fall overboard.

As we pulled away from the pontoon I felt very anxious and tense. I tried to remain calm and happy, and stayed busy by keeping the younger children away from the sides of the boat. Then the man called out to me. He wanted me to come up the front to sit on his lap and help him steer the boat. Somehow I knew that this was not just a casual thing, like sitting on your father's or mother's lap – there was an urgent tone to his voice that gave him away. I instantly froze, then heard inside my head: *'Keep calm, joke with him and tell him you can't because the little ones might fall overboard'*. I repeated this aloud and tried to appear strong, calm and in control.

He insisted that I come up to the front of the boat to be with him. I knew that this did not feel right, so I held my ground and refused to go to him, while inside my head I heard, *'Stand your ground, don't show him any fear and tell him that he has to turn the boat around because the parents are waiting'*. It felt like an eternity before he angrily gave in. He must have decided that I was a stubborn girl and not to be messed with.

This was the second time I had experienced such a strong feeling and heard a warning in my head. Little did I know that I was beginning to reconnect with my spirit guides. They were warning me of danger and, sure enough, a little while after this incident my family found out that this man was a paedophile.

Spirit has come to my aid or given me signs that have saved me more times than I can write about in one book, but that time on the boat was a pivotal experience I will never forget.

At the time, however, I filed that strong feeling and the voice I heard away in my memory and moved on to my teenage years. As I developed into a teenager, I felt not only my hormones changing, but also my sensitivity to the world around me. I would grow very angry and frustrated in large crowds and could not understand why I didn't feel right. I became a very difficult teen who would not conform.

During this time my parents divorced and my family split apart. I attended three high schools in as many years before ending up at an all-girls Catholic boarding school for years 11 and 12. There, my gifts came in handy because I always knew who I could and couldn't trust. I knew when I could sneak out and be back before lights out and I also knew

which teachers I could wrap around my little finger and which I should stay away from.

My first real experience of dealing with death and grief came in that first year at boarding school, when I shared a room with a girl whose mother was dying from cancer. She was an only child and was boarding because her father could not care for her while her mother was so close to death. We became instant friends as we had so much in common: no home, an absent mother (hers through illness, mine through divorce and distance) and a father who was emotionally just trying to cope.

We would stay awake for hours talking about life after death. With our young minds, we tried to work out what would happen to my friend's mother when she passed. I think this was when I began to realise that I would like to make a difference in people's lives.

It wasn't until I left high school aged seventeen that I felt my spirit guides calling to me again. It started out as a feeling that I should or shouldn't do something, then I began to hear a voice in my mind that would tell me things, the same way I had been warned about the incident on the boat some years earlier.

I began to visit palm readers and market stall psychics but was often unimpressed by their abilities and wondered why they wouldn't give me specific information. It was always very general and could apply to just about anyone.

I ended up learning to use fortune-telling cards and started doing readings firstly for myself, then for my friends and work colleagues. They were delighted with the accuracy of the readings, so my confidence grew. I began to collect many different oracle and tarot card decks.

Meanwhile life continued normally with lots of hard work as I was trying to progress in the world. I had been dating a lovely man for a couple of years and one day I decided that I would get my future read to see if I would marry him. I had heard of an interesting teahouse in the city where you could buy a cup of tea and have a reading, so I booked an appointment for me and a couple of my workmates. We excitedly headed into town on our lunch break.

I remember walking up the steps of the teahouse thinking that it was a bit old, dusty and spooky. I thought to myself, 'I hope the tea and cakes are fresh at least, because I'm starving.' As we walked in, I noticed that there were three areas curtained off. Each of us was shown to our own private area for our personal reading. It was a bit unnerving, but exciting too.

I sat down in front of a little old lady with long, straggly grey hair. She seemed quite ordinary and not at all scary. Then I noticed that she had her eyes closed as if she had fallen asleep. I thought to myself, 'Great, my thirty minutes will be filled up with a sleepy old lady!' The next moment her eyes popped open and she said very loudly, 'Who is Toby?' I almost passed out. That was my boyfriend's name.

I told her about him but she just shook her head and told me I would not marry him. She went on to describe who I would marry. My time with her ran out and I remember thinking, 'Well, she got Toby's name right but pity about the other stuff she got wrong. I *will* be marrying Toby, I know for sure.'

However, as it turned out, everything this amazing medium had told me was right – the man I would marry, his appearance and personality, were all correct. I didn't remember what the medium had said to me until after the birth of my first child, Lachlan, with my husband at the time Adam, the very man she had described to me.

This whetted my appetite for spirituality once again, and I began to gather as much information as I could about tarot card reading, angels, spirit guides and the afterlife.

I discovered an online spiritual community that had groups for psychic readings and development. These communities consisted of people from all walks of life and from all over the world. Every day I would make time to visit these online communities. I learned new skills from listening to others giving and receiving psychic readings live in the chat rooms. I began to meet the same people each day in the same community room, which became my training ground for spiritual mediumship. Gone are the days of the village elders, wise ones or medicine people handing down their spiritual truths and lessons. In this online community we all felt connected as one in the search for spiritual growth.

The spiritual community chat rooms were very busy with up to 30 to 40 people in them at once. One day I decided to provide readings live in the open chat room. I got out my fortune cards and started to read for anyone who was interested. They seemed very happy with the results and I quickly became known as the one to ask for a free card reading.

My gifts became stronger each day as my confidence grew and the number of people I read for increased. However, after a year or so, I grew tired of everyone's demands for attention and free readings, so I had a break from the online spiritual community. After quite some time I decided I would like to learn more about Spirit and the universe before I read for anyone else. I searched through the other online communities until I found just the right one, called Spirit Guides.

I loved the energy there. I was usually the only Australian as most of the people were from the USA, Canada, UK and New Zealand. Many were great healers and psychic mediums who were also trying to find a place to rest and share without the demands of having to read for everyone all the time. It was in Spirit Guides that I met an amazing woman who changed my life forever. Her name is 'Ten Feathers', she is from the USA and she is a Native American from the Lakota tribe.

Ten Feathers is a naturally gifted medium who worked for many years as a psychic profiler with the police. She is also a metaphysical teacher who has helped many people to connect with their passed loved ones. I spoke to her nearly every day and she helped me to understand my psychic abilities and explained what each sign I received from Spirit meant, and what I should do about certain information I received.

As time progressed, Ten Feathers began to encourage me to access information from the spirits of passed loved ones who I felt or saw around the people I read for. She encouraged me to communicate with these spirits so that I could pass on any messages from them to their living relatives. It was easy for me to talk with the spirits, as they felt just as real to me as the people sitting on the other side of the world typing on their computers. I no longer needed to use tarot or oracle cards.

Eventually Ten Feathers introduced me to the next two major mentors in my spiritual development – Lilbearpawwoman and Goldenwolf, a wonderful couple also from the USA and of Native American descent. Both were very gifted psychically.

I began to spend more and more time talking with the three friends. They were like parents or elders to me, and would always advise me on how to handle different energies and what to do with my visions. As a result, my visions became much stronger and I would often need my three friends to act as translators for me because my spirit guides would use Native American symbolism or language that I could not understand.

I used to get cross with my spirit guides and ask them, 'Why must you show me this in Lakota, Sioux or Navajo? You know you can show me the signs in English or in a way I can understand.' But my spirit guides were always stubborn and said no, I had to learn it this way through my three Native American friends.

The visions we shared continued for many years, across the oceans. During this time I began to do readings for people in the online community without using cards. I would just focus on the person's energy and let my spirit guides tell me what I needed to pass on to the person.

I finally became confident enough to begin doing in-person readings again, but this time it was for the general public, not just friends and family members. I advertised in the local paper and started to see people at my home for 'in-person' psychic readings.

As time passed, my work increased and life became hectic with two toddlers and a husband. I ended up seeing clients at home two days a week and flying to Sydney for three days to read for clients there. My whole life was beginning to be a blur. One minute I was in Brisbane reading a little old pensioner in my home office; the next I was flying to Sydney to read a high-profile TV celebrity out of my hotel room.

Something had to give and it was up to Spirit to slow me down. Of course this happened in the most creative and special way they could do it. At the age of 30 I fell pregnant with my daughter. Just as I was achieving a successful career as a professional psychic medium, Spirit granted me my wish to have a little girl to complete my family of two boys.

I was terribly ill with morning sickness all day and night for 20 weeks. It was the pregnancy from hell, and I was in and out of hospital. I realised it was time for me to call it quits on my mediumship and professional readings. My life and that of my unborn child were at risk if I was to continue channelling at such a high energy level, so I cancelled my bookings for the next six to eight months and notified my clients that I wouldn't be reading until further notice. I resigned myself to the fact that I might never be able to read professionally again, but I was happy to be a mum to three beautiful children, as well as a wife, friend, daughter and sister.

Spirit, however, had other plans for me. It is true that once you become a medium your life is one of service. Spirit may give you a break in desperate circumstances of ill health, but you will always be called back to duty when you are healthy again. That is what happened to me. When my daughter was six months old, I began to feel Spirit hounding me again. I tried to ignore them and told them to go away and that I had stopped my spiritual work, but they persisted and I ended up giving in to them. Now I am very busy again, with quite a long waiting list, but my work is so rewarding. Spirit is happy, I am happy and I am grateful that they persisted in encouraging me to go back to work.

I lost contact with Ten Feathers for some time when she became very ill and was unable to access her computer or telephone. However, we did eventually start to email each other again and to this day we catch up with each other on social media sometimes. Lilbearpawwoman and Goldenwolf visited Australia and stayed with me and my family. We regularly caught up via phone and email over the years. Our connection was very strong until they both passed a few years ago. Even though they are both in the spirit world now, I still feel them strongly and receive signs and messages from them.

Lilbearpawwoman and Goldenwolf have even started to come through to some of my students who I now mentor. It is so lovely that they are helping to teach me how to mentor others, just like how they patiently mentored me many years ago. It is always a wonderful surprise when they pop up in one of my mentoring sessions with a student. I feel truly blessed.

My journey towards being a professional psychic medium may not have taken a traditional path, but it was the way Spirit wanted me to learn. In this day and age it is important to use any resource you can to find the information you need, whether it be in books, or via the internet or television.

I hope this book will help you to find the answers to the many questions you may have about life after death.

1

Life on the other side

Why does the spirit have to live on after physical death?

I believe the purpose of life continuing after physical death is for us to grow spiritually. Each lifetime that we spend here on earth, we learn different skills and experience different lessons so we can achieve a greater understanding of the universe and how it works. For us to gain as much knowledge and growth as we can, we must live in a physical body then pass away, go to the afterlife, review our life and choose what lessons we need to learn the next time we want to live a physical life again.

How can I be sure that there is an afterlife when we pass?

Every person has their own beliefs and each of us has our own way of experiencing things. The only way you can be sure there is an afterlife is to experience it yourself, whether through signs or confirmations from your passed loved ones, angels or spirit guides; through a near-death experience; or even through hearing firsthand accounts of other people's experiences.

What does heaven look like?

Heaven looks like whatever the person who has passed wants it to look like. If it felt like heaven for an old man to be sitting on a chair at the end of a jetty fishing, that's what heaven would be like to him.

Each person has their own idea of what feels beautiful or comfortable for them. A mother who loves to have children and family constantly around her might have a home in heaven that looks or feels the same way as her earthly home. She may have spirit children coming to visit her and her passed family members close by.

The one thing that each spirit has told me when they have come through in a reading is that the colours of heaven are so beautiful, vibrant and bright, it is like the sun is shining. It is definitely a place that cannot be adequately described until you see it with your own eyes.

Is there limbo, or purgatory?

I don't believe there is a purgatory. The old-fashioned religious stories of souls being held forever in limbo – a place that is neither heaven nor hell – do not make sense to me.

What would be the point of having a physical life experience and learning all of our life lessons if it was to be wasted, and we were to be left floating in an abyss of energy which never moves forward? These outdated beliefs were originally used to keep people in line, to cause fear among the masses so that they would bend to what the church wanted.

Does hell exist? What does it look like?

Just as I don't believe in the existence of purgatory, nor do I believe there is a place called 'hell'. There is no fiery pit with horned devils tormenting you for all eternity, as depicted throughout the ages.

What I have been shown and told is that there are many different levels in spirit. The people who have lived terrible lives full of hate, destruction, murder and cruelty are sent to a level which is quite like being in kindergarten. They are forced to learn their lessons, and are made to see what they have done incorrectly and what they need to do to help fix the problems they have caused.

These spirits are constantly monitored by high-level spirit guides and angels and are never left alone. The universal light near these spirits is not as bright, warm or comforting as that of the higher spiritual levels of heaven where people have lived full, wholesome lives.

Is there anything I can do to help my loved one in spirit progress spiritually? I don't want to hold her back.

The best way to help your loved one in spirit is to live your life in a happy and healthy way. If you are happy and not holding on to your grief so tightly, she will feel a lot lighter and will have more of a chance to progress to her next spiritual level.

Is there pain on the other side?

No, physical pain does not exist on the other side. There may sometimes be a feeling of disorientation or confusion for the person once they have passed, but no physical pain.

Many times spirits come through in a reading showing a physical complaint that they had before they passed, such as an amputated limb or painful lower back. The reason they come through with their physical ailments is to prove their identity to their loved ones and to ensure they can be identified among a group of other passed relatives. The pain of their injuries is no longer with the person in spirit; it is purely a visual reminder for the person having the reading. Once the person having the reading recognises them, the spirit will immediately become the picture of health, looking their best and happiest. It is very beautiful to see the transformation and the yellow light that surrounds them.

If a person has an intellectual disability in life, such as Down syndrome, will they have the same disability when they pass?

No, they will not have the same disability in spirit. Once a person has passed into the spirit world they return to their pure natural state and are able to fully comprehend everything that has occurred in their physical life. All disabilities are removed.

Often people choose to have a disability before they are conceived and born. As strange as it sounds, they actually wish to experience life with a disability. They and their family members progress spiritually much more quickly by having had such a difficult experience on earth.

Will I be able to remember my life on earth when I pass?

Yes, you will be able to remember parts of your life on earth that were important to your spiritual progress. You may not remember insignificant details, such as who your Grade 1 teacher was at school, but you will remember things that were important to you and your family in life. The painful memories gradually fade away and are replaced with the information and lessons of why those painful events occurred. Sometimes people call this the life review.

Are there any particular tasks that people perform on the other side?

Yes, there are various tasks that people must undertake when they pass into Spirit. These are energetic tasks, such as helping the collective consciousness of the universe, assisting new spirits as they arrive, or becoming spirit guides to family members and friends.

Learning and teaching are the main tasks that spirit people perform. It is very much a self-paced energy that allows the spirit person to review their lives and achievements and work out what they have yet to achieve in future lives.

One task, my favourite, is something I often hear of when I read for parents who have lost young children aged from about seven years up and is that of welcoming other children when they pass. The spirit children take great pride in telling their mums and dads that they are very busy helping the new kids and showing them around. The smiles on their faces and the bright energy they give out as they feel proud of this special task warms my heart whenever I think of them.

Often passed fathers and mothers come through and let their children know that they are busy catching up with relatives who passed many years earlier. They say that they really haven't had time to relax, between catching up with spirit relatives and keeping an eye on living relatives. They sometimes jokingly complain they never get a chance to put their feet up!

What happens to a woman who terminates her unborn child, and what becomes of the child?

The mother who terminates her child will still have to deal with the loss emotionally and physically.

The child's energy will still be connected to the mother and will reconnect with her when she passes.

Do we get to choose who we will be in our next life on earth?

Yes, we get to choose what life experiences we will have to help us learn and grow spiritually. Our spirit guides help us decide which personality traits and physical characteristics we will have, such as sex, height, size and ethnicity.

Every life experience is determined by the physical, material and spiritual choices we have made before we are born into our next life. For example, a female who is born with blonde hair, blue eyes, a trim athletic body and who is living in a rich family in the western world would have a completely different set of life experiences from a female who is born with dark hair, dark skin, a weak frail body and who is living in a poor family in Ethiopia. Each spirit chooses their physical appearance, personality traits and location for a reason.

Can I choose not to come back after this life?

It totally depends on how many life lessons you have already learned and what is best for you spiritually. You may be having a very difficult life experience this time around, but it doesn't mean that your next life will be so hard. You can only decide whether you come back or not once you are in the spirit world and you have been through your life review with your spirit guides.

When people pass, are they still emotionally attached to their material possessions, such as jewellery or property?

From my experience after reading hundreds of different people, most people in spirit do not worry about the material objects they have left behind.

Some spirit people do like to check if their loved ones are surviving financially and that everything was sorted out the way they wanted it to be, for example, in their will. Of course the spirit people know the answers to these questions; they just want to make sure their living relatives know they still care and love them, and can see what is going on in the family.

Jasmine, her daughter and the car

Just recently I had the pleasure of meeting an amazing lady, Jasmine. She was a new client who had come to me for a reading. Jasmine had just turned 40 and was very young looking with a bright, sparky personality.

When I first met Jasmine I thought, 'Wow, she must be on top of the world!', because her energy was so positive. She sat down with me and I began her reading. As I was talking with Jasmine I could feel a strong young female spirit next to me. She kept pointing to the ring on Jasmine's right middle finger.

Because this spirit was so bossy I had to stop what I was saying and ask Jasmine if I could hold the ring. I told her that I had a female spirit with me who was saying it was hers, and she wanted me to hold it so I could talk to her.

Jasmine smiled and, her eyes becoming a little teary, she said, 'Yes please, I was hoping that she would come through and yes, that is her ring.' As soon as I took the ring the female spirit started talking non-stop.

She told me that she was Jasmine's daughter and that she wanted to let her mum know that she was okay. When I told Jasmine this she was overjoyed, and said, 'Yes, that's my daughter Zali.' Zali went on to talk of many personal things that only she and her mum would know. Then I asked Jasmine if there were any questions that she wanted to ask her daughter.

Firstly Jasmine wanted to know if there was anyone else with Zali, and as soon as she asked this I saw a young dark-haired guy come and stand next to Zali. He had a big cheeky grin and he casually put his arm around Zali's shoulders.

I mentioned the spirit guy to Jasmine and she let out a huge sigh of relief. She pulled out a photo and showed me a picture of her daughter Zali and the guy that I had just seen with her in spirit.

Jasmine went on to tell me that the guy was Zali's boyfriend Jamie, who had died two years and one day before Zali. Jasmine was delighted to know that they had found each other in the spirit world, because they had been so happy and close when they were living.

Zali had passed in a car accident caused by a drunk driver when she was just 20 years old. Both Jamie and Zali had passed at very young ages but they were not concerned by that at all. They were happy to be together and joked about the fact that they had both caused enough mischief in their 20 years to last a normal lifetime.

The next question Jasmine asked was what did Zali want her to do with all of her clothes and belongings? Zali whispered to me that she didn't really care much for her clothes, except for one big jacket. She asked me to tell her Mum to keep the jacket because it fitted her and she loved it.

Jasmine nodded and said, 'Yes, I know the jacket she's talking about, and I will keep it because it's mine. Zali took it off me when I first bought it.' She laughed and told me it was a lovely warm

winter jacket that zipped up at the front. She had bought it from an expensive surf store.

Zali didn't mind what happened to the rest of her clothes, whether her mum gave them to a charity or to her friends. She wasn't connected to them at all. But there was one thing that she was very connected to – her car! She had a passion for cars, and was in the process of doing up a car that she loved. She showed me a picture of the car in my mind.

Jasmine knew how much the car meant to her daughter so she asked Zali what she wanted done to finish the car. Zali kept telling me she wanted two colours on the car, and one was a sparkling silver. When I reported this to Jasmine she said, 'Do you mean chrome?' Not knowing much about cars, I realised that was probably what Zali meant. So I confirmed this with Zali and let her mum know.

Zali also kept pointing to the rear window on the left-hand side of the car. I made sure I told Jasmine about this and she instantly laughed and said, 'Yes, that's where her favourite sticker is, a playboy bunny!' I asked Jasmine if she would keep the sticker on the car and she said, 'Definitely.'

What I love about this story, and want to stress, is the amazing strength and grace with which Jasmine has dealt with her grief and the passing of her only child, her beautiful daughter, at such a young age. She now knew her daughter was safe and protected, and she could still feel the connection with Zali. She also knew her daughter hadn't changed – she was still full of life, funny and outspoken.

I also want to highlight Zali's attitude towards the disposal of her clothes. After we pass, we are no longer emotionally attached to our material possessions; we have no use for them in spirit. But sometimes there are a few unique possessions that have a deep sentimental value, such as Zali's car and ring. We may wish to give such significant objects to a particular person to remember us by, or simply to enjoy as we did when we were alive.

2

Passing on

I haven't followed any particular religion or faith; will that stop me from going to heaven?

You will definitely not be stopped from going to heaven, or the afterlife, whichever term you prefer to use. It's very important that you realise each and every person, no matter what faith or beliefs they have, has the same ability to grow spiritually. We are all made from the same Universal Spirit.

Do I have to say any particular prayer when I am passing or do anything that will help me move on to heaven?

This totally depends on what feels right for you and what your own personal beliefs are. Prayers can relax and comfort many people, or they can bore and annoy others. It is up to the individual.

There are no particular prayers you must say or things you must do to get into heaven, or the spirit world. From what spirit people have told me, it is my understanding that there is no gatekeeper who stands at the entrance

to heaven and asks for a secret password or prayer before you are allowed to progress spiritually to the afterlife.

However if someone is at peace within themselves and has, for example, come to terms with a terminal illness, this can help them to progress spiritually more quickly because they will not have to adjust as much to the new energy around them when they pass into the spirit world.

Should I be concerned about whether I am going to be buried or cremated? Which is better spiritually?

When people in spirit come through for readings, often their family members will be stressing out about whether their loved one was happy with the way they were buried or cremated.

Spirit people can be blasé about their answers to this question. They say that they are no longer attached to their physical body, so they are not concerned with what happened to it. They just wanted whatever was easiest for their family to deal with and to remember them by.

There is no right or wrong way to say goodbye to the physical body; it is a personal choice and it does not affect you spiritually. For example, if someone was lost at sea and their body was never found, they aren't held back spiritually and it's no harder for them to go to the afterlife. It also does not mean someone with an expensive funeral with all the trappings gets further ahead spiritually. The spirit has no need for the connection to the physical body once it has passed.

Funerals, cremations and memorials all have one thing in common. They are all very important ceremonies which allow grieving family members and friends to experience closure and to say a last goodbye to the physical body of the person who has died.

When we pass, can we see our own funeral?

Yes, we have the opportunity to see our own funeral or memorial service. Sometimes a person in spirit may not wish to do so. They may choose to keep away from that energy; it is a very personal thing. I have had some spirits come through to me raving about how touched they were when they were watching their funeral and how surprised they were at how many people showed up and what was said. Other spirits have come through and have not wanted to answer their loved one's question about what they thought of the funeral. These spirits just shut down and I can almost see them zipping their lips because they don't want to go near that energy; they just want to focus on their new spiritual energy. This is not a bad thing; it just means they may still be dealing with passing over from their physical body.

Who meets us when we pass?

Usually the first spirit person you will meet will be your main spirit guide. Your main spirit guide has been with you from the moment before you were conceived right up until you pass away. Your spirit guide will help you with your transition into the spirit world, where you will be met by passed loved ones and pets.

When someone passes, the family on earth grieves and may hold a goodbye ceremony such as a funeral or memorial. It is the opposite for the person's family in the spirit world – they hold a welcoming party! They are happy to reconnect with their loved one and are excited to show them all the wonderful things that can be experienced in the spirit world.

Do we remember the circumstances of how we passed when we die?

Yes, often spirit people come through to me in readings telling me exactly how they died. They even share who was with them, the date or time that they died, and where it happened.

Sometimes the details they share can be quite graphic. They may visually show me the exact injury they sustained to their body, which can be very hard for me to see, particularly if it is a child or young person who has passed due to a traumatic event or accident. When this happens, I have to be very careful what I tell the family member sitting in front of me.

They may also show me physically how they died, which is difficult because they can get carried away with making me feel it energetically in my own body so I understand. An example of this is when someone has passed from not being able to breathe. I will suddenly feel my chest go tight and it is like I cannot breathe myself. It can be difficult to explain to a family member why I'm suddenly coughing with watering eyes and trying to gain my breath. It is easily fixed however. I just tell the spirit to step back and ask them to calm down, explain that I understand how they passed and that I will pass the message on to their loved one if they back off a bit so I can breathe.

Passing is not always a traumatic experience. Some spirits smile peacefully and tell me that how they passed is no longer a concern to them, they are just so happy to be where they are now.

Other times a spirit person will not want to talk about how they passed because they would rather spend time talking about happy things.

What happens if someone passes in tragic circumstances?

When someone passes very quickly or tragically, whether it be by their own hand (suicide) or by someone else's hand (accident or murder), it can take them a while to adjust to being in spirit. Each person is different so it depends on the individual, but usually it takes time for them to get their bearings and to work out what the next step is for them spiritually.

If they were not ready to pass, or they were mentally unstable before they passed, they are sent to an area in spirit where they are monitored, nurtured and looked after by other passed loved ones, friends and spirit guides. It is almost like a spirit hospital, where their spirit can regroup, re-energise and begin to adjust to their new way of life in the spirit world.

Many times they just need to be in a state of sleep or deep trance and peace to allow them to recharge, to be able to understand what has gone on and why they are no longer living in the physical world.

My loved one was struggling and angry when he was passing away in the hospital bed. Does this mean he won't be at peace now that he has passed?

Even though your loved one was struggling and fighting for his life, it does not mean he is not at peace now.

Please also see the previous answer because it may apply to your loved one too. He may have needed a short time in a relaxed, nurturing environment to adjust to his new life in spirit.

If someone is on life support or in a coma, is their spiritual body still attached to their physical body or have they already moved on to heaven?

Often the person's spirit has already left their physical body, so only their physical body remains in the hospital bed.

There are also times when a person is still connected to their physical body; they are in a state between the two worlds where they can drift in and out of the physical world. They can be visited by their spirit family, angels and guides, and they can also hear and sense their physical family in the hospital room.

These people have a choice of whether they permanently pass and go to the spirit world or whether they return to their physical body, recover and progress with their life on earth.

My friend took his own life. Will he be in hell now? Is there any chance that he is okay?

People who suicide do not go to hell or any evil place as some may believe. As I said in an earlier answer, there is no hell, just different stages in the spirit world.

When someone suicides, they are looked after by their passed family members and spirit guides, and are shown what impact their actions have had on other people around them. Your friend may have to repeat some of his life lessons in his next life so that he can continue to advance spiritually and complete the original tasks he was sent to do.

Felicity, Jack and Bob

Felicity had come to me for a reading in the hope of connecting with her family members who had passed away. At the beginning of the reading I had asked Felicity not to give me any details as I wanted to look and see what I got first and pass that on to her.

Felicity is a mother of three grown kids. During the reading I gave her information about her two older children. As we talked about each one, she showed me that child's photograph.

Finally we came to the photo of her third child. There was a photo of him as a young boy laughing on his dad's knee. And there was also a second photo – of him as a teenager with spiky hair, smiling and looking 100 per cent handsome and ready to cause mischief wherever he went. Now, Felicity and I had not discussed exactly who she wanted to connect with, but as soon as I saw her youngest son I knew he was who we needed to talk to.

I was quite surprised, however, when I felt an older male jump in to speak to me first. He kept pointing to the photo of the younger son and his dad. So I listened to what he had to say. He told me that he was Felicity's husband and that he had their son with him.

I took a deep breath, preparing myself to tell Felicity this, then I explained what had just happened. For a moment she didn't say a word, then she looked straight at me and said, 'Yes, that's my husband Bob.'

I went on to tell her, 'He says he has your youngest son with him.' She was very quiet again, and then she said, 'Thank goodness that he has him and they are together!'

It's hard to put into words how extremely emotional it can be to reconnect couples, and parents with their children.

Bob went on to confirm various details with Felicity about their marriage together. He wanted to let her know how proud he is of her and what she has had to go through alone. He also wanted her to know it was about time she found another partner because she needed to share her life with someone again. 'She's not 80 years old,' he said, laughing. Bob helped to calm Felicity down with his jokes and in doing this she opened up a lot more.

When she was relaxed enough he brought through their son. He was such a wonderful energy, so loving and happy, very youthful and excited. The first thing he said to me was: 'Tell her "Jacky Jack".' I did so and she laughed. I asked what it meant and she told me his name was Jack.

He then proceeded to mime playing a guitar with his leg kicked high in the air – this was him playing air guitar, he told me. I passed this message on to Felicity. She laughed again and said, 'Jack was always doing that. He loved air guitar and silly Kung Fu moves.'

It was wonderful to reconnect Felicity and Jack because their love and bond was so strong, and because Jack was a great entertainer and loved an audience.

After a while Jack settled down and wanted to apologise for what he had done to his family. He told his mum he was so sorry for leaving her and for taking his own life. He tried to explain to her that he was not thinking straight and it was nobody's fault.

No one could have known that he was so depressed because he was so good at hiding it behind his happy act.

Jack had been just 18 years old when he suicided. His death affected so many people in his community, as well as friends and family. Jack had been met by his father who had passed 12 years before him.

I asked Felicity if she had a question for Jack and she wanted to know if he was now happy.

Jack excitedly bounced around and brought through a young female spirit he called Michelle. He was very proud to tell his mum that he had met someone since passing over. She was a similar age to him and she had passed by her own choice as well. She had passed through anorexia.

Jack wanted his mum to know that he and Michelle had so much in common and that they were enjoying sharing time together in spirit. He was very happy and didn't want her to worry so much about him missing out on having a girlfriend and getting married.

When Felicity heard about the girl Michelle she was delighted. She confided that one of her biggest regrets was that Jack had never had a real girlfriend or experienced a loving, intimate relationship before he passed.

'He's more than making up for that now,' I told Felicity. In the spirit world, love is not physical; it is a transfer of energy. She laughed and the weight of the world seemed to have lifted off her shoulders after we finished talking with her husband and son.

Even though Jack took his own life, it did not separate him from his father who had passed by natural causes. He was not stuck in a negative mindset or 'hell' where he would be imprisoned forever;

rather, he was nurtured and encouraged to look at what his actions had caused. But suicide is never the answer to a problem and Jack will have to come back eventually to revisit and relearn the lessons he didn't complete this lifetime.

3

Connecting with loved ones in Spirit

The day he went away

It is important for me to do the job I do. My life as a psychic medium does not stop at 3 pm when I finish my readings at the office; it continues every day, wherever I go and with whoever I meet.

Sometimes I wish I could just turn Spirit off and tell them I want a night to myself to just be me – but this rarely happens. I have lost count of the number of times I have gone to a party, christening, wedding or even just out to a pub, and Spirit has come up and butted in. I am used to this now and have come to terms with the fact that my life is one of service.

I believe there are no coincidences in life, so it makes sense that sometimes I am at a particular place for a reason, so that someone's loved one can come through. It may also be because the person I am talking to needs answers to questions they have long been afraid to ask, until they meet a complete stranger who they feel comfortable talking to – me!

One comment I often receive is that it must be great to be able to talk to my passed loved ones so easily whenever I want to, since I can talk to everyone else's. But this is actually not the case and people are often shocked to hear that I cannot connect with the one person in the spirit world I would really like to talk to on a regular basis – Nonno, my Italian grandfather.

Nonno was the only man around me who never raised his voice or spoke angrily. He was the strong, patient driving force in my life, who loved me for who I was, no matter what crazy thing I had done. He would just sit quietly with a look in his eye that made me think about what I had done. And he would calmly say things to me that made such practical sense. He never demanded that I do something or forced me to his way of thinking; everything was always a suggestion.

Being such a strong, healthy man, I thought my Nonno would live right up until his 100th birthday. So it was a shock when, in his early 80s, he suddenly became ill. He was diagnosed with cancer only six months before he passed away. It was a very aggressive cancer which had spread throughout his whole body. When the time came for him to be hospitalised, I made sure I was there with my grandmother every chance I could. It was hard because I had two young sons, but I knew this would be my last opportunity to spend time with him in this physical life.

My family are strict Roman Catholics, so it was difficult for me to break the ice with him about my work as a medium. When he was awake and alert I joked with him and told him he could talk to me when he passed as that is what I do for a living, and he would need to know that everyone would be all right here.

In the last days of my Nonno's illness, I sat with him and watched as he struggled for breath while he slept. It was very hard for me to understand why Spirit had to take him in such a painful way. As the time drew near to his passing, I knew he was unwilling to leave his physical body. I could see him in his lucid state fighting with his parents in spirit, saying he did not want to go. This was

painful to watch because I knew it was inevitable that he was going to pass from this life to the next. I begged my spirit guides, passed family members and the Archangel Michael, our family's patron saint, to help him calm down and accept that he needed to pass and not be afraid.

On the last day I saw Nonno, I held his hand and said to him, 'I love you, please listen to me. It is beautiful on the other side; please don't fight it any more. And if you can, please let me know you have arrived safely and are happy where you are.'

Although he was very weak, he smiled slightly, and as I kissed him goodbye I saw a tear slide slowly down his cheek. I knew this would be the last time we would speak in this life.

He passed the following day, early in the morning when those at his bedside had left briefly to get coffee. He was such a proud man; I knew it would be hard for him to pass while everyone was standing around him. It is often the case that people choose to pass in the minutes they are alone.

I received the phone call at about 9.00 am. My husband at the time and I packed up the kids and left them with a babysitter, then drove silently to the hospital. On the way I remember looking at the sky, thinking it was such a wonderful blue. There were no clouds and the sun was shining brightly. I wondered how it could be such a beautiful day when the world had just lost such a gentle, special man.

The cars buzzed around us as we drove through the city to the hospital. I was thinking to myself, 'How can they be driving like this and getting in our way? Don't they know we have to hurry up and get to the hospital to say goodbye before my Nonno is moved away?'

When we arrived, the hospital's energy seemed completely different from the day before. The place felt much smaller – claustrophobic – and the energy was heavy. I walked past a group of nurses who were in the tearoom, laughing and joking. Again I thought, 'How can they be laughing when Nonno has just passed away?' It seemed as if the world had stopped for me but continued for everyone else.

When we walked into the room, I saw my family standing around the bed where Nonno lay. I walked up to his body and felt the coolness of his skin, and the grey colour made me wonder where he was, because this was not him. I kissed him on the cheek and then it hit me that he had already left. It was as if a light switch was flicked off. I still felt the grief but I wasn't emotionally attached to his physical body.

On the drive home I didn't want to talk, so I switched on the radio. The first song to play was Wendy Matthew's 'The Day You Went Away'. The lines that stood out for me were:

Hey, there's not a cloud in sight
It's as blue as your blue goodbye
And I thought it would rain
The day you went away.

As I listened silently to this song, I heard my guides telling me to remember it, as it was for me and my grandfather. I was cranky with my guides so I just huffed and said, 'Yes, okay, whatever.' I didn't realise until much later how much of a sign this song would become for me.

Months passed and I began to wonder why Nonno had not contacted me. I thought perhaps he had not heard me ask for a sign from him. It wasn't until one day I was visiting my grandmother when I noticed the old clock on the wall in their TV room had stopped. This clock had been there for years and always ran on time, so I commented on it to my Nanna. She looked up at the clock and told me it wasn't the only one that wasn't working. Another clock had stopped too, as had her special watch. They all showed different times but had all stopped within a very short period. I smiled and told my Nanna that this was the first sign from Nonno – he had made the clocks stop.

As I drove home that day I turned on the radio and what should come on but the Wendy Matthews song. 'The Day You Went Away' has not been a hit since the 1990s and the radio station was not the kind that played golden oldies. I knew this was another confirmation from Nonno that he was all right.

It never ceases to amaze me how spirit people come up with the kind of signs that they do. Over the next few months, whenever I felt particularly upset or angry, I would hear 'our song' on the radio, whether in the car or at home. I even heard it in shopping centres. It was always reassuring to know that Nonno was still there.

Another sign came in the form of a dysfunctional garage door at my Nanna's home. The electric door had been my Nonno's pride and joy. He got a great kick out of pushing the button on approach and driving straight in under the house without having to get out of the car. The door was not very old and had never had a problem before, but one day, a few months after Nonno passed, it got stuck halfway down. Nanna called my husband at the time to see if he could fix it. He tried everything but nothing worked, so next Nanna called in an electrician.

When the electrician came out and touched the door, it opened and closed instantly; there was nothing to fix, which baffled everyone. My Nanna was annoyed to have to pay the callout fee, but it was great for me as I realised that it was another sign.

Six years went by since Nonno passed. For a very long time I received no signs from him and I wondered if he had progressed further spiritually and no longer felt the need to let us know he was all right. I was going through a very busy and stressful time in my life and was almost at the 'What's the point?' stage, when another sign came – and it was the most creative one of all.

I was rushing around getting my three kids ready for school and day care. We were running late and I was becoming extremely stressed. After dropping my boys at school and my daughter at day care I realised that, in the rush, I had left my mobile phone at home. I can't survive without it in my business, so I raced back home to pick it up. As I drove up to my house I noticed a car in the driveway where I would usually park. Frustrated, I pulled up at the kerb, then realised the car in my driveway was a taxi. Just then, the driver stepped out of the car and approached me. I almost passed out: an elderly man, he looked extraordinarily like my Nonno.

Quickly I pulled myself together. The taxi-driver asked me if this was number 41. When I said it was, he told me someone at my home had called for a taxi to take them to the airport. I explained that no one would have called because there was no one at home, and that we didn't need a taxi. He drove off, and as I quickly ran upstairs to retrieve my phone, I suddenly smiled.

It was another sign. The man looked so like Nonno and the airport represented my ability to fly high spiritually and connect. The moral of this story is that signs come in different shapes and sizes. Expect nothing, but keep your eyes open – and say 'Thank you!' when you do receive something, no matter how small.

Can our passed loved ones communicate with us?

Have you ever been alone at night, perhaps sitting on the couch watching TV, and suddenly felt that you are not really alone at all, that someone else is watching you or is simply in the room with you? You don't feel scared; rather, you feel comforted, and you know that this energy feels familiar – like that of a family member or friend. Physically you can feel them there but practically your sceptical mind is telling you that, because you can't see them, they can't be there; it's just your imagination. But I can tell you that it is possible to feel, sense or even hear your passed loved ones in spirit.

You do not have to be a professional psychic medium to connect with passed loved ones in spirit. You just need to learn how to be aware of signs and be open to the possibility that your spirit does not die when your physical body does. It continues on and is able to access greater spiritual understanding in the afterlife.

What sort of signs should I look out for?

Signs from the spirit world or from passed loved ones come in many different ways. It might be just a small sign, such as the lights flicking on and off whenever you think about or talk to a particular loved one who has passed away. Spirit people are made up of energy, so it is possible for them to manipulate electrical equipment such as lights, clocks, televisions, radios and phones.

Another common sign may be a physical object that is repeatedly moved or knocked over, even though it is heavy and no one has been near it. For example, a photo frame, ornament, cross or even a picture on the wall. It takes a lot of energy for spirit to move physical objects, but they can do this. It is not to scare you or make you feel uncomfortable; it is merely to let you know that they are there. I have had books fall from the top of my bedroom wardrobe and open up on just the right page with information I needed for that particular time. However, if your loved one isn't moving physical items, please don't feel upset with them. It can take a lot of practice to learn and master how to manipulate their energy in the right way.

Some other common spirit signs are white feathers being left in front of you or on the floor in obscure places where birds would never be; constantly finding coins as you walk along; and butterflies, birds or dragonflies that seem to linger and follow you.

Certainly you need to be careful not to assume that every little thing that happens is a sign, but it helps if you are open-minded and accept that there might be a reason these things are occurring around you.

If I'm not a spiritually minded person will that stop me from connecting with my passed loved one?

It doesn't stop you from having a connection with your passed loved one, as long as you are open to the process. Whatever their spiritual beliefs, each person has their own method of connecting spiritually, and there is no right or wrong way. As long as you are willing to let go of any preconceived ideas and give it a try, that is all Spirit asks.

I am Roman Catholic and am worried that my priest and the church would not agree with me trying to connect with my passed loved ones.

Only you can decide whether it feels right for you to connect with your passed loved ones. Having a psychic medium reading may not suit you, but praying for your passed loved ones, thinking about them or even talking to them either in your mind or out loud, might bring you much comfort.

You may like to check with your local priest on this subject, but I am sure he will agree that whatever feels right for you will be right for the church as well.

Is there any particular thing that I can do to help me communicate more clearly with my passed loved ones in spirit?

The best thing you can do is try to leave your expectations out of communicating with your loved ones. Try not to force yourself to see, hear or feel things. You may not be able to hear your passed loved ones or see them physically, but you may sense or feel them around you.

Having a clear mind and taking time out to slow your thoughts with meditation can help you be more open to receiving messages. Eating, sleeping and getting your body moving also helps because if your body is tired, hungry and sore it will be difficult for you to have a clear mind.

Little signs are always present; it is up to you to learn to decipher what is a sign and what is not. Trust your instincts and notice things that happen out of nowhere and are repeated to you in various ways.

I can't bring myself to go and visit my father's grave, it is too painful for me. Do our passed loved ones get angry with us for not visiting them at their final resting places?

No, they do not get angry at us for not visiting their final resting place. You can connect with your loved one's spirit anywhere, any time. You do not need to go to a cemetery or memorial. The important thing is that you are acknowledging your loved one. They do not want you to be distressed, they want you to be happy and at peace when communicating with them.

How often should I contact my loved ones in spirit?

You can talk to your loved ones in spirit whenever and wherever you wish. You will not drain them by simply connecting with them through your thoughts or feelings, or by talking to them.

It is a different story if you are constantly trying to connect with them through a psychic, medium, healer or Ouija board. Please see Chapter 8: Psychic Mediums and Spiritual Readings for more information.

Can departed loved ones hear our thoughts or do we have to talk to them out loud?

They can hear your thoughts because you are telepathically linked. Some people prefer to communicate by talking out loud; others are more private and will talk with their thoughts. It is totally up to each person and what feels right for them.

Katrina, Sam and the number 3

I had read for Katrina once before. That time, her son Sam had come through as clear as a bell. He was very loud, and so impatient that he was waiting for me even before his mum's appointment time. I loved talking with Sam because he was so specific with details to prove to his mum that he was still around and that he could see what was going on with his family.

Sam had told me that the number 3 was very significant. He also said that he had made the CD player at his funeral play the same song three times to get everyone's attention. When I relayed this to Katrina, she said he was right: the CD player had been stuck on the same song at the funeral and no one could fix it. At the time, Katrina had wondered if it was Sam but she hadn't been sure.

Sam also told me he lived at number 3, and that the number was very important for his mum and dad to know. Puzzled, Katrina said that they didn't live at number 3 so she wasn't sure what it referred to. I told her to write it down because it might make sense in the future. The fact that Sam kept repeating it meant that the number 3 was to be important in some way.

That was about six to eight months earlier. Sam had passed not long before in a freak mountain accident. He was barely 20 years old.

Recently Katrina booked in for another phone reading. I knew that Sam would be strong but I had forgotten how powerful he actually is. While I was waiting to call his mum that morning, I was trying to figure out my mobile phone – I wanted to change the ring tone on it as I was tired of the current one. Out of nowhere I felt a male presence arrive; he was young and full of energy. He came and sat next to me. I could feel him staring at my mobile and what I was doing. At first it was off-putting, but then I realised who it was: Sam. He had come early to wait and speak to his mum.

He was not at all impressed with some of the music I tried as a ring tone. It was just like a bossy younger brother trying to play with my mobile. I was thankful when it was time to call his mum.

I told Katrina about the mobile phone incident and she laughed. Yes, she said, that would be Sam – he loved gadgets. She went on to tell me that she'd had the most amazing experience since we had spoken last.

She asked me if I remembered telling her about the number 3 and that Sam had said he lived there. I did, and I was so surprised by what she told me next.

Katrina and her husband had ordered a gravestone for Sam from the stonemason at the cemetery. When the stone arrived, Katrina and her husband were shocked to see a huge gold '3' above Sam's name. As they had not requested this, they were amazed. The gravestone had been ordered before Katrina's previous reading when Sam had insisted that the number 3 would be important to them. When Katrina rang the stonemason to find out why the number was there, he had no idea. He said that Sam was buried in row 3 at the cemetery but it was not the norm for the cemetery to put the row number on the gravestone – in fact, no other gravestones had such a number on it.

This big gold 3 was a sign from Sam. Katrina reminded me that Sam had said he lived at number 3 and, she added, he was right. He does now live at number 3 in the cemetery.

This was a big sign from Sam to show his family that he is still around them and he loves them very much, so much that he would go out of his way to make a visual sign for them.

4

Family

David and Naomi

When Naomi first walked into my office I thought, 'Gee, she looks nice.' Naomi was a young woman aged about 26 with blonde hair and blue eyes and she was wearing a pleasant summery skirt and top.

I could tell from the look on Naomi's face that she had been through a lot. She was nervous about being in my office. After a few minutes of chit chat as I explained what usually happens in readings, I began to feel a strong male energy enveloping me.

This male energy was full of excitement and love for Naomi and I knew he was definitely a partner or boyfriend who had passed over. As usual in my readings I began to tell Naomi what I was feeling, that there was a male energy wanting to talk to her and it felt like he was from the same generation as she.

He was expressing his love for her.

Naomi tried her best not to cry or show any emotion. Even though it was hard for her, I continued to relay the man's messages. Finally Naomi broke down and told me that this was David, her partner who had passed.

David went on to talk about their little girl, Suzie. He told Naomi how proud of her he was and that she had been doing a great job raising her. 'She has always been a wonderful mother and nurse,' he said. After confirming some more personal information, I noticed the energy in the room began to shift. Naomi felt it too.

I knew that David must have been working up to a big message for Naomi. I took a big deep breath and said to him, 'Hit me with it!'

David explained that he didn't want Naomi and his little girl to be lonely and to live by themselves without anyone looking after them, so he had sent someone to Naomi.

Naomi listened quietly while I continued. David went on to say that the new man's name was the same as his, and that his birth date was very important as well.

With this information, Naomi began to squirm in her seat opposite me. I told her that I was almost finished with the message and asked if it was all right to continue. She nodded. I felt David's energy strongly around the room.

I was quite emotional at this stage as well because I could feel how much love David had for Naomi and vice versa. I held it together and gave the last message from David, which was: 'I have loved you ever since we were young, that is why I have sent this man Dave to you. He is the upgraded version of me and now you can dance with him like you never could with me.'

At this point Naomi lost it. She was blubbering on the couch and I was tearing up too, so we both used tissues. Naomi took a deep breath and said, 'I love you too, David, and thank you. I will keep telling Suzie about how great you were and what a wonderful daddy you were to her and how much you loved her.'

After delivering his message, and hearing Naomi's response, David was finally at peace to go. The energy in the room shifted to a calm, serene energy and Naomi let out a huge sigh. It was as if the weight of the world had been lifted from her shoulders. Naomi then told me her story:

David and Naomi met when they were 19 years old. He was wild, funny and loved fast cars. She was studying to be a nurse and they fell in love quickly. Naomi thought it was great being with David because he knew how to have fun.

They were together for a while before Naomi fell pregnant. David and Naomi were thrilled to be having a baby. Their little girl Suzie was born and she meant the world to them. After a few years, however, they went through a stressful time and when David and Naomi decided to split up, it was hard on all of them.

After being separated for a while they began to try to work things out. They were in the process of getting back together when David was killed in a car crash. Suzie was only five years old.

After David passed Naomi didn't want to date, or even look at anyone else, but there was a guy she met who wanted to be friends. His name was Dave, which was too close to home for Naomi so she pushed him away. He was persistent though and after being friends for some time, Naomi let him in and they fell in love.

Now I forgot to tell you the other important thing about Dave. He was born on the same day as David. This scared Naomi as well. She worried that she was just trying to replace David. But her family and friends were very positive about the relationship, despite the weird coincidences of name and birth date.

Naomi then told me that she and Suzie eventually moved in with Dave and she soon fell pregnant. She and Dave had a little girl, Emma, a baby sister for Suzie.

I asked Naomi about David's reference to dancing. Smiling, she reached into her handbag and pulled out a photo. She said, 'I didn't want to show you this at first because I wanted to see if he would come through.'

I looked down at the photo as she handed it to me; it was a photo of David. He had beautiful blue smiling eyes, sandy hair and he was seated in a wheelchair. He could not walk or dance! He had never been able to walk or dance: he was paralysed from the waist down.

I smiled at Naomi, gave her a hug and said, 'You must share this with Suzie and Emma when they are older, because you are all now watched over and protected by a very special man called David.'

Will I be able to meet up with my loved one who passed 50 years ago or has it been too long now?

Time means nothing in the spirit world, so 50 years is like the blink of an eye. There are no time limitations so it doesn't matter if they passed six months or 70 years ago. If they are waiting for their family members, they will still be there when you pass. See also the next answer for information about reincarnation.

Would it be possible for someone who has died to be born back into the same family (reincarnate) within a short period of time?

It is my understanding that most spirit people wait for four to six generations of their family members' passing so the family group can meet together in spirit again.

After the family group has reunited and each person gone through their life review, they each decide, with the help of their spirit guides, what particular role they will have in each other's lives in the future, such as a friend, teacher, lover, mother, son or father.

In saying this, however, it is possible for a family member to be born back into the same family, but it is less common. Usually a person would only return to the same family very quickly if there is a higher purpose and a lot of unfinished emotional business.

My sister and I had not spoken for years before she passed. I feel guilty about this. Will this stop her from wanting to be around me and my family?

Definitely not! Your sister would have the advantage of seeing and knowing what her life lessons were. She would know that what went on between the two of you was part of both her and your own spiritual growth. Your sister would only want the best for you and your family. She would want to be a part of your life from the spirit world and help you and your family to achieve your goals in this life until you meet up again in the future.

I have two people in Spirit who have passed. How can I be sure that they are together?

Just as we here on earth enjoy spending time with our loved ones, our loved ones in Spirit also enjoy sharing love and time with other spirit people, whether family members, pets or friends.

Even if two people passed quite a few years apart they can still be together. There are no timelines in spirit; they can be reunited whenever and wherever they desire. Often in a reading with a psychic medium, people will come through together to let their family members know that they are not alone. If one person does not have as much energy or passed a lot earlier than the other, the stronger energy will come through first and allow the other person's energy to 'piggyback' on their energy until they learn to communicate for themselves, or are strong enough to sustain the energy.

Can my passed loved one see everything I do, including private moments?

This is such a common question I am asked by my clients, particularly young men and women whose parents or grandparents have passed. The answer is no, your passed loved ones have no wish to see you in the shower, on the toilet or with a romantic partner.

Your passed loved ones do not need to be constantly around you. They do not see you in the flesh; rather, they tune into your energy and feel your vibrations. So please don't feel embarrassed or worried that your passed loved ones can see 'everything'.

Can we meet our ancestors and loved ones in the afterlife?

Yes, we can meet up with our passed loved ones and ancestors. As I mentioned in an earlier answer, usually many generations of the one family will wait together to reincarnate as a group. Not necessarily in the same family dynamic, however; they may come back as friends, teachers, partners and so on.

Please do not worry that your loved ones won't be there to meet up with you. It is rare for a passed loved one to come back in physical form quickly. It may take a couple of hundred years before the family group as a whole or part will decide to return to the physical realm to learn more lessons.

A person in my family who I did not like and who was abusive to me has passed away. Will he be able to connect with me or hurt me from where he is now?

No, he won't be able to connect with you or hurt you. If you don't want his energy near you, you have the free will to stop him from coming near you. He will be working on himself spiritually to amend any pain that he has caused you or anyone else. The best thing you can do is send him forgiveness from your heart. I know how painful this can be but it's important for you to release yourself from him.

I often smell cigarettes in my kitchen when no one else is in the house and no one has smoked. The cigarettes smell like the kind my father used to smoke. Why is this happening?

Often spirit people will leave a particular scent around a person to attract their attention. It may be the smell of their favourite perfume, cologne or flowers. In your case it is the smell of your father's favourite cigarettes. This is just a physical sign to let you know that he is around you and is okay.

My mother was not buried as she wanted to be. I feel guilty that it was taken out of my hands and I could not fulfil her wish. Is she upset with me?

Usually spirit people don't worry too much about their funerals, cremations or memorials. They would much rather you spend time remembering the happy times you shared with them.

Sometimes people have specific plans or wishes that they feel their family must fulfil once they have passed. However when the person actually passes, they realise it doesn't matter so much where they are buried or what colour the flowers were at their funeral. All that matters is that they are now safe, happy and working towards learning higher spiritual concepts and lessons.

I want to move homes but I am concerned that my husband, who has passed away, won't be able to find me and his spirit will stay in our current home. How can I let him know that I have moved?

Spirit people can find their loved ones wherever they go, even if they move homes. If your home is filled with love and happy memories, your husband can still access those memories after you move. He will want to go to where you are, not to the physical address of where you lived.

If I never met my grandparents will they still be around me in heaven?

Yes, it does not matter if you have not physically met your grandparents or other passed family members; they are still attached to you energetically in spirit with your family bond.

I am a widower and wish to know what happens if I remarry. When I pass, will my wife be angry with me, and who will I end up with if both of my wives are in spirit?

I am often asked this question. There is so much love in the spirit world and no jealousy or anger. You can choose to spend time with both of your wives. Unlike on earth, spirit people can have romantic love for more than

one person at the same time, because it's not an earthly physical love with restrictions. It is an energy transfer of spiritual love.

Your deceased wife would want you to be happy, not lonely. I am sure she will be waiting for you with a big embrace when you pass. Enjoy the rest of your life. You do not need to be lonely or feel guilty for being happy.

If my family members who have died love me so much, why don't they ever help me? I feel so lost and alone that they aren't here.

Your passed family members are constantly around you, especially in times of need. However, if you are feeling depressed and overcome with grief, it can be difficult for you to feel their presence.

When someone is sick, tired, depressed or on heavy medication or drugs, for spirit people it can be like hitting a brick wall energetically. If emotional walls are up, it can sometimes be difficult for the spirit family to come through clearly to deliver messages or signs.

Why won't my departed wife show herself visually to me? I ask her and pray constantly for her to appear to me.

It takes an enormous amount of energy for a spirit person to show themselves visually, and can take a lot of time and practice for them to learn.

Perhaps your wife has not learned how to manipulate her energy yet, or perhaps she may not be showing herself to you visually for another reason. She could be worried that you may freak out if she did actually appear in front of you. Spirit will only give us information and signs that we can handle. They don't want to scare us or make us uncomfortable.

Just because your wife hasn't shown herself to you visually, it does not mean that she isn't around you or giving you signs and messages in other ways.

I can sometimes hear my name being called and it sounds like a female voice similar to my grandmother's. Could it be possible that she is calling out to me?

Yes, it is quite normal to hear your name being called. It's possible that this could be your grandmother in spirit calling you, or it may be your spirit guide.

Usually your name is called when you need to pay attention to something. For example, if you are about to cross a road and you hear your name called, you will stop. Perhaps the next moment a truck races past. If you hadn't stopped, you would have been hit and injured.

I hear footsteps at night and it feels as if my husband is still checking the doors are locked before we go to bed. Could this really be him?

Yes, spirit people have been known to carry out their regular routines. They check the doors at night or sweep the kitchen floor, anything that was important to them. They may not physically turn the locks or sweep the floor, but you may hear the noises these actions make or feel the energy. Don't be afraid, it is just your loved one letting you know he is still around and protecting you.

My twin has passed away but I feel him near me constantly and I hear him in my head, as if I am thinking for both of us now. Is this normal?

This is quite common. I have read for a few clients whose twins have passed. Not only are twins sometimes physically the same, as with identical twins, they are also telepathically linked. Sometimes this link does not end when the physical body dies, but it continues. It can be hard for people who have never experienced twins in their lives to understand this.

A twin link is powerful and important for both siblings. The spiritual lessons they undergo in life are often shared with their twin from a young age and it is a very special relationship; even if the twins are separated throughout their lives, the link remains between them. This link can sometimes drain them. If one twin is sick or depressed, it can be hard on the other twin; however everything that occurs happens for their greater good.

Mark and John

I would like to share with you a true story of twin connections, which I experienced through reading a client a few years ago. This client and his reading stand out as one of my most memorable. I will never forget him and his twin brother.

Mark was an identical twin whose twin brother John passed unexpectedly when they were only in their mid-forties. John's passing was a complete shock to the whole family, especially for Mark.

A few months after John's passing, Mark booked in to see me for the first time.

Mark's reading was booked for 11 am one Saturday. As usual I looked at my booking list on the Friday night to see who I was reading the next day. When I saw Mark's name I felt a strong connection with it, but as it was very late, I didn't think much of it at the time and just went to bed.

The next morning as I was getting ready for work I felt a very strong energy around me. This spirit's energy was hyperactive and bouncing around trying to get my attention. I knew that it was a male energy and he wanted me to hurry up and talk to him.

Now just because I am a medium, that does not mean I have to talk to spirits every minute of the day, but sometimes they do get a bit excited or anxious and they try to jump in before their loved ones show up for a reading.

I told this male spirit, 'I would really love to chat with you but can you please come back in a few hours, or whenever your loved one is coming, to talk to me?' I explained to him that he would not miss out – I promised I would talk to him when I arrived at my office. This must have made him feel better because the next moment I felt the hyperactive, anxious energy leave and I could continue getting ready for work.

Later that morning I read my first two clients and all went smoothly, but just as I was getting ready for my 11 am appointment I felt this whoosh of hyperactive energy enter the room again. I knew then that this male spirit was here for my next reading, with Mark.

When Mark first walked in I was shocked to see a very large man with his head shaved bald, tattoos and dressed like a biker (there is nothing wrong with this look, I have tattoos myself). The reason I was shocked was because I saw Mark walk in twice: there were two of him.

As soon as Mark sat down I began to see why this energy was so persistent; this was Mark's identical twin brother. I smiled to myself and began to tell Mark about what had been going on that morning with this male energy who would not leave me alone. Mark smiled; he wasn't surprised at all. He didn't tell me anything except to verify that this was indeed his identical twin brother John.

It was an amazing experience.

Each time John told me something from spirit, I would start to pass the message on to Mark but before I could finish speaking, Mark would have already acknowledged what I was about to say and answered John. Mark could hear and feel John as clearly, or even more clearly, than I could.

Mark wanted to confirm with someone else that he was hearing John and that he wasn't crazy. The brothers would have a conversation with me and it was as if the two of them now shared one body. I said this to Mark and he very calmly told me that when John died, it was as if a part of his spirit moved over to make way for John's spirit to enter his body. He went on to say that he sometimes thinks and feels for both of them.

The love between the two brothers was a beautiful thing to witness and was so strong that it will never be broken. It was so personal for Mark that he didn't share this connection with John with just anyone; he would only share with people who understood. To everyone else Mark was just the same person he'd always been.

I have never seen Mark again but it was an honour to have met both Mark and John. I am sure those two biker brothers are up to mischief somewhere.

5

Children

Alex, Melissa and baby Talia

A little spirit girl came and visited me one day at my home. She was about the size of a two-year-old toddler, with curly blonde hair and beautiful hazel eyes. She was very small and bubbly.

At first I thought that maybe one of my children had accidentally invited this spirit child into our home but then I realised that she wanted me to pass a message on for her. She told me that she wanted me to talk to her mummy and daddy for her. I said to her I would try to, but I needed more information so that I would be able to find them and know that they were her parents.

She smiled at me and said that I would know who they were when I saw them. She hung around me and my home on and off for two or three days. This didn't bother me as she was doing no harm, and she was a sweet, bright little energy.

After a few days she went away. I forgot about her and her message because I was so busy. Not long afterwards, I was doing readings over the phone and was getting ready to call my next client when the little girl showed up in my office. I tried to smile at her and tell her that I would talk with her later, but she was really impatient and just stood in front of me. By this time I couldn't communicate with her as I had already started to talk to my client.

The little girl was jumping around trying to get my attention, when my client, a young man, asked if it was okay to put me on speaker phone so that his wife could hear also. I agreed and began the reading. Suddenly the little girl was yelling, 'That's my mummy and daddy!' I was hesitant at first and I didn't want to feel silly because these clients hadn't said they wanted a mediumship reading. But I trust my spirit guides and I trusted this little girl, so I said to the couple, 'Before I go any further with this reading, I have to say that I have a little girl with me here who is in spirit. Is it okay if we talk to her?'

There was a gasp on the other end of the phone. I heard crying from both of them. They both said, 'Yes please!' I then knew the little girl was right; these were her parents.

I took a deep breath, crossed my fingers and said, 'She is calling you mummy and daddy.' There was a big sigh down the phone. I let out my breath and quietly thanked my spirit guides for not giving me a bum steer.

I began to describe their little girl to them, telling them that she had curly blonde hair. They were both so happy to hear that – they had always wanted to know what colour hair she had, they said.

I then described her beautiful light hazel eyes, and heard Melissa cry and laugh with delight. She explained that her baby girl had her eyes.

Melissa and Alex went on to tell me that their daughter Talia had been stillborn four months earlier. They had never seen her eyes or hair colour as she was born so early and had never developed properly.

The energy of Talia was amazing – she was an exceptional communicator. I am not sure why she appeared as a toddler to me but maybe that was the easiest way for her spirit to communicate with me.

Talia told her parents that they would have two more children and would be pregnant again very soon. She also said that they were right to move house. They confirmed that they were moving in two weeks and were trying to get pregnant again as soon as possible. They were so excited to have been reconnected with their daughter and were full of positive energy with hope for the future with their two healthy children to come.

Their relief was tangible. They were now able to breathe easily knowing that Talia is a real little girl who is doing really well.

Talia may not have lived very long in the physical world. She may never have taken a breath outside her mother's womb, but she was – and is – larger than life and very much alive on the other side in the spirit world.

If a child passes at a young age do they continue to grow on the other side?

Yes, spirit children do continue to grow on the other side; they experience life and growth just as they would here on earth.

Spirit children have goals they must work towards, specific growth points to meet and lessons to learn. They go through their spiritual life without the pain and suffering or restrictions they had on earth in their physical body.

My child didn't know anyone who had passed away and now that they have passed, I am afraid they are by themselves and lonely.

No one is ever alone in the spirit world. Your grandparents, great-grandparents, spirit guides, angels or other children will be around your child in spirit.

My spirit guides have told me that if a child who passes away doesn't know anyone else who has passed, they will be met by an animal or familiar cartoon character or even Santa Claus. This of course would not really be Santa Claus or Spider-Man or Tinker Bell; rather, it is someone sent to relax the child's spirit and help them to ease into the spirit world. As they begin to accept the new energy in the spirit world the cartoon character energy will fade away and their spirit guides and family members will become stronger around them. They can then spend time with other young spirits and learn to adapt once more to their spiritual life without their physical body.

Will my baby remember who I am if she was only a few hours old when she passed?

Yes, of course she will remember you. No matter how long you and your child were together physically, you will always be connected spiritually. You will meet up with her in the spirit world when you have passed.

It does not matter if a child passed through miscarriage, abortion, stillbirth or any other way, they are all kept safe and stay connected to their family, in particular their mother's energy.

Why do children have to pass? What is the purpose of such a short life?

When a child passes, there is definitely a greater purpose in the child's life and that of their families, friends and parents. The death of a child affects so many people, and this helps each of those people to grow spiritually.

Before we are conceived and born we each decide how and when we want to pass. We decide which is the best way for us to learn as much as we can, and in what period of time we would like to achieve this.

A child who passes may have chosen to experience a short time on earth so they can progress more rapidly when they return to the spirit world.

My daughter was only seven years old when she passed from leukaemia, yet she was so comfortable talking about angels and death. How could this be?

Children are still very connected to the spirit world. It is normal for them to see and feel things with their sixth sense. Usually when a child is talking about their imaginary friend, they are referring to the child's spirit guide or a passed loved one.

Often angels and spirit guides will visit terminally ill people, including children, before they pass; it is a time to reconnect with spirit.

We did not christen or baptise our baby before she passed. What does this mean for her spiritually?

It does not matter if you haven't baptised your child before they pass. As I have stated in earlier answers, Spirit does not favour one religion over another. Even if someone never believed in anything during their life, they are treated in the same way as someone who was very religious. Each spirit, baptised or not, progresses to the afterlife and is protected by passed loved ones, spirit guides and angels.

I often see my child, who has died, in my dreams. Is this really him or is it just a dream?

It is common to see a passed loved one in your dreams. You may see them standing in front of you smiling, but often they will give you messages. Dreams are important tools for Spirit to pass messages on to you, because when you are in such a relaxed alpha state, your emotional walls are down. The way you can tell the difference between a normal dream and a spirit visitation is by the feeling the dream gives you and the details you remember from it.

With a real spirit visitation during a dream, you will wake up feeling relaxed, comforted and as if you have actually seen or been with your passed loved one. You will remember the details of the dream for months or even years afterwards and it will always feel the same; the details won't change.

In a normal dream you may remember some of the details when you wake up in the morning but within a short period of time, perhaps a day or so, you won't remember the whole dream. The details will be foggy or confusing and you won't feel as if you have met with your passed loved ones.

Am I wrong to be relieved that my child is no longer in any pain? After such a long journey with cancer I am glad that he is finally at peace.

No, it is not wrong to be happy that your child is finally at peace and pain-free. It takes a lot of courage for you to look past your own grief to let your son move on into the spirit world. One of the most important gifts you can give him is to allow him to be at peace; it is a wonderful thing to do.

Is it normal to want to still celebrate my child's birthday even though he has passed?

It's very normal to want to celebrate birthdays, anniversaries, Christmas or other special times of the year with your family members. Just because your child has physically passed, it doesn't mean he can't still enjoy the happy times and energy that you give out for him, especially on his birthday.

Grief is an individual thing and what may suit one person may not suit another. You may like to have just a small dinner or gathering in memory of your son's birthday and share a birthday cake together. Some like to release balloons with messages tied to them or written on the balloon. Whatever feels right to you and your family will be fine for your child in spirit also.

Is it acceptable for me to grieve and cry in front of my children?

Yes, your children should understand that it's all right to cry and to feel. You are teaching them a great lesson by showing them how to experience their emotions; to let yourself cry and grieve is a very important thing to do.

However, you wouldn't want to lie on the couch crying hysterically for months and months on end. After releasing and grieving there will come a time when you have to try to move on. It is normal to feel emotions in life, but if your grief is holding your life back, you must look at finding some help. You may like to talk to a grief counsellor, see your local doctor or even visit a support group regularly.

What is the best way for me to tell my child that her grandmother has died?

It is always best to be honest with your child. I know it is difficult to tell a child about death and try to explain what has happened, but just keep it very simple. Make sure you keep the explanation age-appropriate and don't go into too many details that may confuse the child.

When my grandfather passed away I found the best way to tell my eldest son was to tell him the truth. I explained that Nonno had become very sick and because his body was no longer healthy, he had to leave it because it didn't work any more, but that he was still around in heaven watching over us all.

I let him know that Nonno could still hear when he spoke to him and that it's okay to miss him. I didn't stop talking about Nonno after he passed. I would remind my son of the funny things he did or when his birthday was.

A good way to tell your child about dying is to explain that it is rather like having a shirt that doesn't fit you any more. Even if it's your favourite shirt and you want to keep wearing it, if it's too tight, it will hurt if you try to do up the buttons. There comes a time when you must give that shirt away and get a new shirt that fits better. The new shirt will have more room for you to grow and it will not hurt you any more. You will also feel a lot cooler and lighter than in that old, worn-out tight shirt. This is the same with our bodies. When our spirit is ready to move on and our body is worn out or sick, it can be hard to say goodbye to the body but our spirit still moves on to a better energy (a better shirt) that fits perfectly for what we need to grow spiritually.

How does grief affect children?

Each person reacts differently to grief, and it could be in a completely unexpected way. Some children may deal with death by suddenly being full of questions and wanting to know all the nitty-gritty details of how the person passed, what happens to the physical body and where they go once they pass. It can be confronting having to answer all these questions, but this is quite normal as children are very curious. As I said in the previous answer, just remember to keep the information truthful but age-appropriate.

Other children may appear to be dealing with their grief really well until some time later when reality hits as they realise that their loved one will not be coming back to them in the physical world.

Another common reaction is for children to be extremely angry at the world and everything and everyone in it. They may want to hurt themselves or lash out at the people who are closest to them, either verbally or physically.

The best way to deal with grief in children is to give them time to heal and allow them to come to you to talk when they need to. Try not to set exact timelines or hard-and-fast rules about when they must recover.

Changing a child's routine can affect them, so if you can, try to keep things as normal and safe as possible. Perhaps finding a local grief support group or a school or grief counsellor may help you with answers, or help the child to realise they are normal and other people have been in the same situation.

Katie

It is always hard to keep my emotions at bay when reading for a client who has lost a child. Being the mother of three young children, I always find the thought of your own child passing before you do very confronting. This is one of the most painful things that can ever happen to a person in life.

The main reason I continue working as a professional psychic medium is the satisfaction I get if I can give even a glimmer of hope or reassurance to a parent who is grieving after losing a child.

By giving very significant personal details to the parents from their child in spirit, you can see that the love and connection between parents and children never disappears. You can witness the moment they realise their child is in fact still with them and is safe and happy. When I see their smile break through the tears and hear them breathe easily for the first time in a long while, it is worth more than any money in the world to me.

I would like to share with you a memorable experience I had with a grieving family and their little girl, who had passed over and was in the spirit world.

I had just come off the performance stage at the MindBodySpirit Festival in Melbourne. After providing readings on the main stage for random members of the audience, I had gone to the side of the stage to talk to members of the audience who wanted to say hello or ask me a quick question.

The line was quite long and many people were waiting to talk to me. As each person came up, I quickly answered their questions and hoped they were the answers that they needed.

I was nearly at the end of the line and was thinking I would soon have to get something to eat and drink before I began to feel faint, when a group of three women came up to me together. There was an older woman and two younger women, who would have been in their late 20s to early 30s. It wasn't until they were standing quite close to me that I noticed one of the young women was actually being held up by the other two. She was obviously quite emotional and needing her mother and sister to be there as strength for her.

I kept calm and asked if there was anything I could do for them or anything they would like to ask. The woman's sister spoke first, asking if there was anything I could tell them about her sister's daughter. The grief in all their eyes, particularly the young mother's, is still burned into my memory as I write this.

I told them I would see what I could do. Inside my head I called out to my spirit guides and asked them to please give me the extra strength to help these people, as I was worn out from so many readings. Within moments I experienced the familiar feeling of spirit energy around me. It was very strong and I knew that this must be the spirit of a child – their little girl.

I wish I could remember the little girl's name but I can't as it was such a brief encounter; however for the purpose of telling this story I will call her Katie.

I think Katie was about nine years old and she had passed from cancer. She came through with such a strong energy, it gave me the boost I needed. It was as if she had turned on a tap as the information began to flow from her to me.

Katie began by saying that she was really excited about being there and by being able to talk to her mum, her grandmother and her auntie.

She was very specific and kept telling me the name Tam. I asked her what this meant but she said to just say it to her family. I told them the name. Instantly I saw a smile spread over Katie's mother's face. I asked them who Tam was. Katie's mother said, 'Tam is Dr Tam. He was Katie's doctor, he helped her so much and he made such a difference in her life. Dr Tam was Katie's favourite doctor.'

After hearing her mother say that, Katie went on to tell me that she was so thankful for Dr Tam and if her mother ever saw him again to let him know that she was really healthy now and to thank him for all he did. She also explained that it wasn't Dr Tam's fault; he did everything he could have done to save her. When the three women heard this they all nodded and agreed, yes, he had done all he could. Katie's cancer had been so far advanced that no matter what anyone tried, it was inevitable that her body would eventually not be able to cope and that she would pass.

Katie then asked me to remind her mother that she doesn't like the colour pink, like other girls. She loves the colour purple. She said that she was happy that her mother didn't dress her in pink. All three women laughed at this, because it was true; Katie did not like the colour pink.

The minutes were ticking by and there were still a few more people waiting in the queue to talk to me, but I wanted to make sure that Katie and her mother had every chance to connect again, even though it was only for a brief few minutes.

After a couple more personal confirmations from Katie, I began to feel that she was working up to something that would really hit home that it was indeed her and that she was still alive in the spirit world.

Katie asked me to tell her mother that she would never be hungry again and she was so excited to be able to eat all of her favourite foods again now. I passed this message on to her family and they all laughed out loud.

Before Katie passed she was so sick that she wasn't able to eat normal food or even taste her favourite foods. So when Katie passed, her mother decided to assemble a care package with all of Katie's favourite lollies, chips, chocolates and food that she would want to eat, and placed it in the coffin with her. This is why Katie was saying she had lots of her favourite foods with her and would never be hungry.

This was the first time I had ever heard of anyone packing food in with their loved one, but it was such a special thing that meant so much to both the mother and the daughter. It was this small detail that really hit home to Katie's mother that she really was okay.

After passing this final message on to her mother I felt Katie's energy begin to fade. As she left, she laughed and asked me to let her mother know that she would always love her and would always be around her no matter what.

The three women smiled and thanked me for the messages. As they turned and walked away I felt the heaviness of their grief slowly begin to lift. Katie and her family will always be a special memory for me even though it was just a rushed few minutes on the side of a stage. It is these spur-of-the-moment connections that can sometimes be the strongest, because Spirit has gone to great lengths to get a message through to a loved one.

6

Pets

Can psychics or mediums connect with pets that have died?

Definitely, animals have often come through in readings I have provided for my clients. They are just as connected to energy and Spirit as humans are, and are sometimes more intuitive, so it is common for pets to come through.

If you would like to connect to a specific pet that has passed away, make sure you check that the psychic or medium you are going to see does connect with animals, or get word-of-mouth referrals from friends and family members.

Will my beloved pet be waiting for me when I pass over?

Yes, your animals do wait for you. Many times I have seen budgies, cats and dogs all lining up next to a person in spirit. The connection between owner and pet is not severed by physical death; there is still a link of love that keeps them connected.

Is there an animal heaven?

I do believe that animals share the afterlife with human spirits if they choose to. If the animals were wild and did not share their life with humans, of course they may not choose to be in the same energy area as humans. It is up to the free will of every animal or human energy to be where they would like to be.

Can my deceased cat come back to me in this life as another cat?

Yes, your passed pets can come back to you in the same lifetime. On many occasions I have known friends and clients who have had dogs or cats come back into their owner's lives. The pets seem to have an immediate knowing and connection with their owners and sometimes they also have the same fussy eating habits or favourite ways to sleep or play.

It can be reassuring to pet owners to know that their beloved pets are back. If a pet doesn't come back in this life it doesn't mean that they love you any less, it is just that they may choose to help you from spirit, instead of being in the physical form again.

My dog has been mourning for my husband since he passed. Is this normal?

It is normal for animals to mourn for family members and also for other animals. If you have ever looked into a dog's eyes after their owner has left, whether through death or family breakdown, you can see their pain. It's like looking into a person's eyes in the same situation.

Next lifetime can I choose to come back as an animal?

From what I have learned from my contact with the spirit world and my spirit guides, it's my understanding that once your energy level has advanced spiritually to that of a human, your consciousness and energy cannot go back to being an animal.

Do animals sense Spirit or see it?

Yes, animals most definitely sense and see Spirit as they are very attuned to their sixth sense. Animals have their own inbuilt lie and energy detectors and they will instinctively avoid someone who doesn't feel right.

Often an animal will sense or see a spirit before a sensitive human does. Sometimes you may see a dog sitting and staring at nothing, but happily wagging its tail as if it is with a loved one. Or you may notice a dog or cat vocalising or focusing on a particular area in a room, where you can't see anything.

Animals have always had to rely on their sixth sense for survival.

Can my pet come back as a human?

It can take many lifetimes and spiritual levels to progress from living as an animal to living as a human. So in theory, yes, your pet may come back as a human, but it would not be in the same lifetime you are experiencing now.

Will my dog still be able to protect me now that he is in spirit?

Yes, animals are still connected with you after they pass. Instead of being able to protect you physically, he can protect you as an animal spirit guide.

He will be able to give you signs and feelings that will make you pay attention. For example, you may get the feeling that you should not walk down a particular road late at night, or a sense that you shouldn't go to a certain event, then later you find out that something dangerous occurred right where you would have been.

Bundy

I have a client whose German shepherd passed away. Bundy was her protector. My client lived alone and he was always on guard at night so she would feel safe enough to sleep.

Bundy was more like a best friend and bodyguard than a pet. When he passed, my client felt very lonely and frightened to be alone at night without her dog to protect her. She wasn't sleeping well and was at her wits' end by the time she came to me for a reading.

Even before I met this client for her appointment that day, I knew that her reading was important and that a special reunion would take place. While I was waiting for her to arrive I kept feeling a very strong, protective male energy, and out of the corner of my eye I would see a dark shape around the height of my waist pacing back and forth.

I was not frightened by this as I myself have a wolf spirit as a protector, so I knew that this must have been a visitor for a client. Sure enough, he was my next client's much-loved dog.

I didn't want to alarm my client, so after a few minutes of general talk, I gently brought up the fact that she had a special visitor waiting to connect with her, a large, very protective German shepherd. She became emotional and, as per usual, my trusty tissue box was on hand for the tears.

After the tears subsided, my client reached into her bag and pulled out a colour photograph of a healthy-looking, large, male German shepherd lying on a patch of green grass.

Bundy then began to talk to me. Talking to an animal spirit is no different from talking to a human spirit. Each spirit delivers its message to my spirit guide who then translates it to me.

During the reading, Bundy told his owner of many different personal details of their life together. He even highlighted that his back left leg had given way at the end and it was upsetting when he could no longer run or walk with her.

Bundy went on to tell his owner to please not feel bad or worry about him because he could now run wherever he needs to as he has full use of his legs again. One thing that makes me smile is when I remember Bundy asking me to please tell her, 'Mum, the smells over here are amazing!' He went on to say to her that he could see she wasn't sleeping well at night.

My client nodded and confirmed this through her tears. He told her that she need not be scared because he still protects her at night in spirit; he checks on her constantly through the night and makes sure that all is well. Now this does not sound like it would make much of a difference, but to my client it certainly did.

She emailed me a couple of weeks later to thank me for the reading, and at the bottom of the email she wrote: 'PS: I can now sleep through the night again, knowing that I am protected by my Bundy in spirit.'

7

Angels, spirit guides and ghosts

Are angels real?

Yes, angels are real. Angels have been documented since humans first began
to communicate, whether through art, writing, dance or the spoken word.

Angels have been sighted and felt physically or energetically by people of
all ages, ethnicities, religions and belief systems. It can be hard to believe
that they exist if you haven't experienced them yourself or been in contact
with someone who is aware of angels at work in their life.

Is my passed loved one my guardian angel?

It depends on what your own belief systems are and what your definition of
the term 'guardian angel' is. My understanding is that guardian angels are

separate from your passed loved ones; most angels have not actually lived on the earth and had the dense earthly experience.

Your passed loved ones can definitely still look after you and guide you, but they are not the same high pure vibration as an angel. It is totally up to you what you want to call your passed loved ones; the term 'guardian angel' may give you some relief or make sense to you.

Are spirit guides real?

Yes, spirit guides are real. Everyone has their own spirit guides, but some people are not aware that such beings exist, or they are not open psychically to them.

Some spirit guides may choose not to show themselves to you; they may only allow you to hear them in your inner ear, like a thought in your mind. Or they may cause a physical sensation that you will come to recognise as the presence of your spirit guide when you experience it, for example, shivers of cold which make the hairs on your arms and back of your neck stand up.

What is the difference between angels and spirit guides?

Most angels have not had a physical life on earth. They are pure spirit beings, who are made up of a very high energy vibration and who have not been tainted by the earthly trials and tribulations that we all go through as humans. They have specific tasks to perform.

Spirit guides also have specific tasks, but they come from a place of empathy; they know what it is like to have been human because they have experienced many lifetimes on earth.

You may have known your main spirit guide in a previous life; they may have been your mother, brother, sister or friend. Spirit guides work with you to help you achieve a successful life and progress spiritually. They can also help you to call on the higher vibrations of the angels when you need extra help, for example in healing, teaching, parenting or with protection.

What is a ghost?

A ghost is the common name used for an earthbound spirit. Ghosts are spirits which are still attached energetically to particular places like their homes, to objects such as jewellery or to people such as their family members.

Ghosts have been given bad publicity over the years and have been feared by both adults and children. The reason these spirits are earthbound is because they have chosen not to go to the light and enter the next energy phase out of fear, confusion or attachment to the physical world.

The energy around ghosts can sometimes feel very heavy, confused or even frightened, and it can be perceived as being negative.

In my experience, ghosts – or earthbound spirits as I like to call them – are like lost children wanting to go home. You cannot blame them for being confused or not understanding why no one can hear or see them. They need help to be shown to the light so they can be happy and move on spiritually.

Ghostbusting

Recently I was called to an old Brisbane mansion which had been converted to a wonderful office space. Some of the staff had been frightened by a spirit presence in the building – three staff members had felt and heard someone, or something, walking around in their boss's office.

As soon as I heard about the situation I asked my spirit guides what was going on. They gave me two clues about what I would be dealing with if I went to the building. The first thing that was shown to me was an older male spirit; the second was my sign for the back corner of the building. I decided that it would be a good idea to go and have a look at the office, and an appointment was made for me to visit the office and talk with the staff.

A few days later I did my usual preparation for spirit removal. I found the tools I needed to take with me on this type of so-called 'ghostbusting' visit. I made sure I had four small amethyst crystal points, some white sage incense and my protective space-clearing spray – which I've developed to help me clear out negative energy.

When I pulled up in the front of the heritage building, which was in an inner-city suburb, the first thing I noticed was the inscription on the front: BUILT IN 1888. We were greeted at the front door by the personal secretary to the boss, who was also the owner of the building. The boss himself was working offsite that day.

As we walked into the old mansion I took in how beautifully it had been restored. It retained all its old-world charm but with the added benefit of the most up-to-date technical equipment. The place was a hive of activity.

I asked the secretary if I could take a walk through the building first before I spoke to any of the staff. The first place I wanted to go to was the far back corner of the building because, according to my spirit guides, this was where the spirit would be.

As I approached the corner, I began to feel a male spirit's energy. I reported this to the secretary and she nodded, telling me that was where her boss's office was – the office where staff members had experienced something. I then spoke to two of the staff.

The first, a woman, said she had felt the energy at night when she was alone in the building. She was often so scared that she wouldn't go near the back corner of the building and she was reluctant even to stay long enough to turn the computers off.

I asked her if she felt the spirit was male or female. She said she hadn't thought about it before, but now that I mentioned it she thought it was a male energy. I then told her that I could see an older male spirit, who had owned and lived in the mansion previously. He was in the back office and would often pace up and down and around the room. He would look out the back windows at the surrounding houses and the beautiful view of the city.

As I was talking, another staff member came up to us. He was a young guy who said he had heard loud footsteps and chairs being dragged around in the boss's office. He worked in the office below and definitely felt that it was a male spirit, because the pacing had a heavy male tread.

I repeated to him what I was feeling, and he told me that a previous owner of the mansion had also owned a big old brewery, which was visible from the boss's office.

This gentleman was said to look out from his bedroom window (in what was now the 'haunted' office) to check that the brewery stacks were smoking. If there was no smoke coming out, it meant that no work was being done and he would race down the hill in a fury to see what was going on.

While I was talking about the male spirit I started to see and hear two female spirits who were back in a kitchen area. The female spirits were not angry or mischievous; they were just chatting to each other and laughing.

I decided I had better tell the staff about these other spirits, so I explained what I felt – that the female spirits were not a threat or cause for concern – and they were okay with the spirits being there.

However the male spirit was a different matter. He was scaring the staff, and he had no tolerance for female workers in his home. At night his energy would be felt by any women working there. In fact, the staff told me that they had a young female cleaner who had worked for them for years. She now refused to clean the building at night because she was scared of the boss's office.

The spirit showed himself to me as a short, stout, bossy man. He didn't mind the workers being there during the day so much, but after hours was a different story.

This spirit showed me that he was very lonely in life and had passed at about 65 years of age due to his heart and lungs. When I relayed this to the staff, they commented that their boss had started having the same health problems and that he was now

60 years old. They also told me that their boss was short and stout and in the past few months had become much more stubborn and angry, which was out of character for him. It was then I realised that their boss might have been unconsciously absorbing the spirit's energy, which was stuck in the back office.

This is quite an uncommon situation. There has to be a common link or an emotion that the living person and spirit person share. In this case, the spirit felt attached to the home and resonated with the new owner and his business.

Each man had similar roles in life and a similar desire to succeed. The spirit would have become confused and sometimes felt as if he was the actual living person. He might have taken it upon himself to help out or add his own opinions without the living boss even realising it.

I warned the staff that their boss might feel that he doesn't have long to live, since he was now 60 and the spirit had passed at the similar age of 65. They told me that their boss had written a timeline already and had said to them that he felt he didn't have much longer to live.

It made sense that he would feel this way if he was absorbing the spirit's energy. I asked them to pass on what I'd said to their boss and stressed how important it was for him to understand what was happening. I also asked if they wanted me to send the former owner's spirit to the light, so that he could move on spiritually and the boss could enjoy his life and feel better. Or I could leave the spirit in his current state.

They were worried about the ethics of sending the spirit on, but I explained it was fine as long as you are helping the spirit rather than harming it. I left it up to them – and they decided to ask their boss what to do.

I went on to put a protection safety grid around the boss's office, using the four amethyst crystal points that I had brought with me. I asked the woman who had felt the spirit the most at night to come with me. We placed one amethyst point in each of the four corners of the room. This grid forms a safe, protective and soothing energy in the room.

The next thing I asked my helper to do was to spray my protection space-clearing spray in each of the four corners of the room while saying aloud with emphasis: 'I now remove all negativity from this room.'

This was to lift the energy in the room and to clear out any old negative energy. This would not send the spirit away or to the light, but it would calm the energy down until they decided what they wanted to do.

I left instructions that their boss should move out of the back office as soon as he could while a decision was being made. I also advised them to use the protection spray in all four corners of the room every night, and they agreed to do this.

A few days later the secretary called to ask me to return and move the spirit on. Her boss had decided it was best for the spirit – and for him – if the spirit was sent to the light.

The next day I went back to the office, taking with me three white tealight candles, a purple protection candle and the protection spray. I went straight to the back office and was pleased to find the boss there. He had taken all my advice and was happy to help us.

After disconnecting all the computers in the room, we again sprayed the four corners of the room while asking for all negativity to be removed. It was especially important that the boss sprayed the protection spray in each corner and in a commanding voice repeated the words: 'I remove all negativity, I release you in love and light.'

I then asked the boss and the two women who had helped me on my previous visit to join hands in a circle with me. We lit the three white candles first and placed the purple candle in the middle. I explained that the room might get very hot but not to be afraid and to keep holding hands.

The energy began to build up in the room and I reminded the others to be firm and help the spirit go to the light. I then spoke out loud to the spirit, telling him it was time to move on now; that he was no longer needed in this home and that there were far more important and wonderful things waiting for him in the light.

The spirit was resisting so I asked the boss to repeat his earlier words. Then the spirit indicated that he wanted to tell the boss something.

He told me a name to pass on, which I did, asking the boss what the name meant to him. He replied that it was the name of his oldest friend – someone he'd known for over 30 years. The spirit said that the boss must reconnect with this friend and remember to not become too much of a loner.

The spirit then told me he regretted not having made time for anything but the business while he was alive, and he had often felt isolated and alone. He also told the boss that he needed to remember what happened in his life 13 years ago, and how important that was.

The boss looked at me as I relayed this to him and said he couldn't remember anything that happened back then. Then one of the women exclaimed, 'Your daughter was born 13 years ago!' The boss smiled and said, 'Ah yes, my princess. She was born then.'

As soon as the boss acknowledged that, I felt the spirit's energy shift and become lighter. He asked me to tell the boss that family always comes first and never to forget that – don't be alone. A very emotional energy was coming through and as I looked around I noticed that the woman who had felt the spirit the most was crying.

I thanked the spirit for his help. The boss thanked him too, and promised that he wouldn't forget. Then the spirit put a smart black hat on his head, tipped it to me, and walked off towards the light.

Sometimes all it takes for a spirit to move on is a little encouragement or the need to feel they have done some good in their life before they leave.

After I explained what I had seen, we all let out a big breath and I carefully snuffed out the candles. (It's very important not to blow the candles out; as it causes the energy to scatter. If you snuff out the candles, the energy is contained.)

The room felt lighter. The boss came and gave me a big hug. When I left the building I left behind a smiling boss, a staff member still crying from emotion but also relief, and a secretary busily getting on with her day.

I followed up a few days later and they were all happy to say that they hadn't felt the spirit's energy since that day.

8

Psychic mediums and spiritual readings

Can I ask for a particular passed loved one to come through to me in a reading?

You can ask your loved ones in spirit to come through prior to the reading. It is best not to tell the medium who you want to come through at first; that way you are not giving any extra information to them.

It's important that you realise you cannot directly call a specific spirit to come forward; whoever needs to come through in a reading will. Someone who you may not even think of may come through and deliver a very powerful message.

Try not to be too disappointed if your passed loved one doesn't come through. Everything happens for a reason, so perhaps the person you wanted to come through stepped aside so that the other spirit person could deliver their message first.

I am the biggest fan of John Lennon; will I ever be able to contact him through a medium?

I am often asked questions like this. The short answer is no. The only reason John Lennon would come through for you is if you are somehow connected to his friends or family.

When a famous spirit person has come through in a reading that I have given, it has always been for a specific purpose related only to their own personal family or friends. They do not need to connect with strangers or people who are trying to connect with them out of pure curiosity.

Of course, all situations are different and it does not mean that you would never be able to contact a famous person in spirit, but from my experience it is best if you just connect with people who are known to you or your family.

How long should I wait before I contact a medium to help me try and communicate with my friend who passed away?

This is a very personal thing. I have had people wait years before they feel ready enough to come for a reading to connect with their loved one in spirit. I have also had others who have connected within a few weeks.

You need to make sure you have gone through the grieving process and are feeling emotionally well enough to go for a reading. Remember, a reading cannot take the place of the grieving process, but a good spirit connection through a reading can give you hope and relief in knowing that your friend is still with you and doing really well.

I have had a reading with a person who said they were a psychic medium but it didn't feel good to me. The reader didn't tell me anything that made sense. Why do I feel so let down and negative about the experience?

Unfortunately many people claim to be psychic mediums, but be aware there are a lot of phoneys and con artists out there too. It's very important that you know what to look out for when you go for a reading.

Firstly you should never feel sick, depressed or negative after having a reading. The medium should help you feel uplifted, comforted, and reconnected with your passed loved ones and inner spirit. The reason you may feel let down is that perhaps you were not given any of these feelings or any information that could confirm your loved one was truly communicating with you.

Here are a few hints on getting an accurate and reliable psychic medium reading:

- If possible, go to a medium who has been recommended to you by someone you know and who you have heard good reports about.

- Don't give too much information to the medium. Let them tell you.

- Be open to receiving any information; try not to put up emotional walls.

- The medium should give you very specific information during a reading, such as family names, dates or other personal details.

No two readings will ever be the same, even if they are with the same medium and client. It will be unique each time.

My mum has been constantly calling psychic phone lines and booking in to see a medium regularly since my dad passed away six months ago. Is this healthy and normal?

I encourage my regular clients to come every six to twelve months or so, not under six months (unless some big changes are occurring around them in work, love, health, family, etc.).

If someone regularly attends readings every few weeks, this can be very draining for them. It is important for them not to give away their inner power to others by constantly asking for reassurance every day or week; they must learn to trust their own intuition and inner guidance.

Seeing many different healers and readers in the same time frame can confuse a person because they are being exposed to many different energies and information.

Is it a good idea to use an Ouija board to connect with people in the spirit world?

I would never recommend using a Ouija board to connect with spirit people. It can be extremely risky and dangerous to use Ouija boards because you have no control over which spirits you invite in and who you are communicating with.

It is far more beneficial for a person to work one-on-one with their own spirit guides or passed loved ones, without having to rely on other people's energies in a group environment such as a séance with a Ouija board.

Many times a negative spirit or lower entity will appear and they can be extremely mischievous and can attach themselves to the people who are attending the séance.

I have had quite a few clients who have come to me for a reading complaining about being extremely tired, depressed and feeling that someone is always watching them and holding them back. Usually, once I begin to look more deeply into the client's aura or spirit, I can see why this is happening. They have a lower entity or dark spirit draining them.

Straightaway I ask if they have been using a Ouija board or trying to cast spells without knowing exactly what they are doing or watching their intent. Often they will deny it, but occasionally someone will admit to using one. They are usually really young and just messing around for fun.

It is hard to explain unless you have seen it for yourself, but this kind of attachment does happen. It is important that you always work with spirits who are of the light and love, and control who and what you are speaking to.

Is it true that I should protect myself psychically with white light before I connect with the spirit world?

Yes, it's important to protect yourself energetically before you do any spiritual work, whether it is a healing, reading or even just for general daily activities.

There are many different ways to protect yourself psychically. For example, you can imagine yourself standing under a beautiful waterfall. As the water flows down over your face and your body, you are covered by a healing white light energy. The water washes away the negativity and leaves you feeling cleansed and protected.

My favourite way to protect myself and my family is to imagine a large pink bubble in front of me or my family member. There is a zip in the front of the bubble and you must see yourself or your family member unzipping it and climbing inside. Once you are inside the pink bubble you are protected. Do up the zip and know that nothing can come inside without your permission.

Imagine that the bubble is filled with and surrounded by white light, so any negative energy will bounce off the protective wall of light. The bubble is pink because that is the colour of love, so anything that tries to drain you is bounced off with love. Also, pink does not shine as brightly as white does, so your energy does not stand out as much to negative entities.

If someone doesn't come through in a reading does that mean they don't love me or are angry with me?

Definitely not! Just as some people here on earth are quiet, shy, stubborn or private, some spirit people are the same. Perhaps your passed loved one doesn't want their personal business aired publicly with a stranger.

Your loved one may also still be recuperating and will need a little bit of extra time to adjust their energy before they come through in a reading to you. It doesn't mean they won't give you other signs or be with you.

I suggest you maybe wait a while before having another mediumship reading then maybe you could try another medium or even go into the reading without any expectations. This may take the pressure off you and your loved one, and make it easier for them to come through to you.

If a person has high expectations or is very nervous or stressed, it can sometimes make it harder for a spirit to come through. It can feel like the spirit is being bounced off an invisible barrier or wall.

Try to relax and imagine yourself full of light and pink love energy, and say to your loved one in spirit that whatever needs to be said will be said, and there is no pressure because you know they are there and that they love you. This may help you also.

Is it draining for passed loved ones to come through in a reading from Spirit?

Yes, it can be draining for passed loved ones to come through for a reading. If they are trying to break down energy walls put up by their loved ones, it can take a lot of their energy and make them tired.

During a reading the spirit person has to lower their energy vibration and the medium and client have to raise their energy vibration. If a reading or spirit connection goes for too long it can be draining on everyone.

The medium who is giving the reading should know when the passed loved one's energy is starting to become tired or pull back. You should never try to force a spirit person to keep connecting.

My father did not speak English. Will this make it difficult for him to come through to a medium who doesn't speak his language?

No, it doesn't matter what language a person spoke when they were alive. I have had many people of different nationalities and speaking different languages come through.

The medium's spirit guide will deliver the right symbols and messages for the medium to understand, no matter what the language spoken is. Sometimes different names or words in the spirit person's own language do come through in a reading but it is more for a confirmation than anything.

What is the difference between a medium and a psychic?

I am both a psychic and a medium. A psychic is a person who can intuitively pick up information about the client in front of them; for example, past, present and sometimes future information.

A medium is a person who connects with the spirits of the clients' departed loved ones and spirit guides, and passes on accurate information to the client to prove there is life after death and that the spirit still lives on. They can also pass on helpful information about past, present and future.

Most mediums are also psychic, in fact all the mediums I know are. Not all psychics are mediums, however.

Karen and Heather

You might think that all psychic medium readings are very similar, but what would you say if I told you that I have connected in readings with people who have not yet passed away?

A few years ago a young woman, Karen, came in for a reading with me. She had booked in for a psychic predictive reading, which focuses on the client, predicting the future for them and their living family and friends.

While I was reading for Karen I felt a young female spirit's energy in the room with me. She told me she was Karen's friend. I reported this to Karen, but she had no idea who it could be as she had no friends who had passed away.

So I described the spirit to her, mentioning that she had long brown hair and that she was still insisting she was Karen's friend, but the description meant nothing to her. It was obviously important for this spirit to get through to Karen so I began to ask her more questions. The spirit told me that she was very sick and she wanted to say a big thank you to Karen for coming to visit her and keep her company. She said she was in between worlds and that she had not yet passed on.

This blew me away: it was the first time I had communicated with the spirit of someone who was still alive. I let Karen know what the spirit was saying and it was as if a light bulb went on in Karen's mind.

She told me that her friend Heather was very ill in hospital, in a coma. Heather was Karen's best friend and flatmate. A few weeks earlier, she had gone home and found Heather unconscious on their lounge room floor. No one knew what had happened to Heather because she had not regained consciousness.

Heather came through and confirmed her identity. Then Karen urged me to ask Heather what had happened to her – how did she get hurt? Heather told me that she didn't know what happened; it was as if there was a big bang in her head and then everything went black. When Karen heard this, she told me the doctors thought that Heather might have had a brain aneurism.

Meanwhile, I was wondering why Heather was coming through to her friend in this way. There was an urgency about her need to connect with Karen. And when Karen asked me whether I thought Heather would regain consciousness and get well again soon, I had to be honest: I told her that I could see Heather was torn between staying in our physical world or moving on to the spirit world.

As I was telling Karen this, Heather quickly spoke up, asking what Karen was doing at 3 pm that day. Karen told me that she was due at the hairdresser. When Heather heard this she seemed to panic and she said very loudly to me, 'Please, please ask Karen to come to visit me instead.'

I passed this message on to Karen, who looked a little puzzled but agreed to go and see Heather that afternoon. After that message was passed on to Karen, Heather's energy began to fade. The last thing she wanted to say was to thank Karen for all she had done; she wanted Karen to know she felt they were more like sisters than

friends and that she loved her very much. Karen asked me to tell Heather that she felt exactly the same way.

A few months later I saw Karen again. She told me what had happened to Heather. At 3 pm on the day of the reading, Heather decided to end her struggle between the worlds and quietly passed away into the spirit world with her friend Karen beside her. Karen was glad that she missed the hairdresser that day.

As this story shows, connections or readings aren't always the same. If someone is in a coma or has dementia they spend quite a bit of time in the spirit world, so they can communicate spiritually just as passed loved ones do. Heather and Karen taught me so much and I am so grateful for their connection that day.

A final word

As you have seen throughout this book, there are many different signs or feelings that people can experience from their passed loved ones. Each person on earth and in the spirit world is an individual, so we each experience things in our own way.

What I want you to take from this book is the possibility that life does indeed exist outside of our physical world. Personally, I know that it exists from my numerous encounters with spirits on the other side. It is up to you to find your own stance on what you believe.

I do want you to be gentle with yourself, so please do not feel upset or let down if your passed loved one hasn't shown up in front of you or sent you a sign that you have recognised yet. This does not mean that they are not around you; it can mean that you may not have recognised the signs yet or that they are still learning how to communicate or send messages from the other side.

Please remember to live in the present physical world as well. As much as we want to reconnect and spend time with our passed loved ones, it's important to *live* this life, as we are still alive. Be true to your loved ones here on earth and in spirit, and continue to grow, laugh and love.

Thank you for taking the time to read this book, many blessings to you and yours.

Jade-Sky x

Acknowledgements

This book is dedicated to my Nonno, my grandfather; the one man in my life I could count on and who loved me, no matter what.

In no particular order I would like to thank all of the people below for being in my life; for sharing, laughing, crying and moving through life's experiences.

To my children: thank you for being the light in my life, and for teaching me what love is.

To my husband: thank you for your love and support and for being the amazing warrior that you are. The children and I are truly blessed to have you in our lives.

To Hannah, my soul sister: thank you for always being there for me through thick and thin in this life and in many other past lives.

To Richard Martin: thank you for being my friend and manager, and for helping me with my business for all of these years. You are a life saver!

To Lisa Hanrahan, Paul Dennett, Katie Stackhouse and all the team at Rockpool Publishing: thank you for your professionalism and support in making this book.

To each and every person for whom I have read, or who I've come across, who has asked me a question about life after death; to my clients; and to the special people in this book who have let me share their stories: thank you!

And last, but not least, to my spirit guides and the passed loved ones: thank you for all that you do to bring the messages through.

About the author

Jade-Sky is a psychic/medium – a 'direct channeller'. She was born with a special gift of being able to connect clairvoyantly with energies of deceased loved ones. Over the past 24 years she has fine-tuned her natural skills in the areas of tarot and oracle card reading, psychometry, mediumship/channelling and uncovering past lives.

Jade-Sky has read professionally for thousands of clients around the world, who testify to her accuracy.

Mediumship is Jade-Sky's passion. During a reading she offers up key names, dates and specific events to the inquirer so that they know without doubt that their passed loved ones or spirit guides/angels are with them. She also provides very personal and significant details to help clients reconnect with their loved ones, something which assists with their grieving process. By giving detailed information, Jade-Sky reassures her clients that life after death does exist and a beautiful place awaits us when we pass from this life to the next.

Jade conducts private readings and workshops. Jade-Sky's products include *Psychic, The No Excuses Guide to Soul Mates* and *Divine Directions Cards*.

She is based in Brisbane, Queensland.

JADE-SKY.COM.AU

NOTES

NOTES